PARSONS ON THE ROSE.

A TREATISE ON THE

Propagation, Culture, and History of the Rose.

BY

SAMUEL B. PARSONS.

NEW AND REVISED EDITION.

ILLUSTRATED.

NEW YORK:
ORANGE JUDD AND COMPANY,
245 BROADWAY.

LOVEJOY, SON & CO.,
ELECTROTYPERS & STEREOTYPERS,
15 Vandewater Street, N. Y.

PREFACE.

In offering a new edition of this work, the preparation of which gave us pleasure more than twenty years ago, we have not only carefully revised the garden classification, but have stricken out much of the poetry, which to the cultivator may have seemed irrelevant if not worthless.

For the interest of the classical scholar we have retained much of the early history of the Rose, and its connection with the manners and customs of the two great nations of a former age.

For many interesting facts in the History and Culture of the Rose, we are indebted to Deslongchamps, Vibert, Laffay, and several anonymous writers. To the former we wish most fully to express our obligations, both for the plan of this work and for many interesting facts and researches, to which we cannot conveniently attach his name in the body of the work.

Upon the classification we have bestowed much thought, and although we do not feel quite satisfied with the system we have adopted, it is the best that occurs to us in the present condition of rose culture. The amateur will, we think, find the labor of selection much diminished by the increased simplicity of the mode we have adopted, while the commercial gardener will in nowise be injured by the change.

In directions for culture, we give the results of our own experience, and have not hesitated to avail ourselves of any satisfactory results in the experience of others, which might enhance the utility of the work.

We do not claim exemption from criticism in any form, and readily express our willingness to be ever open to conviction, in a field where, among the varied results of experiment and skill, there is much room for difference of opinion.

For our labor we shall feel abundantly compensated, if the republication of this work shall in any way tend to produce a more general admiration and increased culture of the most beautiful flower known. S. B. P.

CONTENTS.

CHAPTER XI.

CHAPTER XII.

CHAPTER XIII.

CHAPTER XIV.

CHAPTER XV.

CHAPTER XVI.

PARSONS ON THE ROSE.

CHAPTER I.

BOTANICAL CLASSIFICATION.

The Rose is a shrub or dwarf tree, with mostly deciduous foliage, and large, beautiful, and fragrant flowers. Its branches are slender, almost always armed with thorns, thinly furnished with leaves, which are alternate upon the stem. Its leaves are pinnate, and vary in color and character, from the rich, dark green, and somewhat rough leaf of La Reine, to the glossy smoothness and rich purple edge of Chromatella. The blossoms are variously arranged at the extremity of the newly formed branches. The calyx is single and tubular, swelling at its lower part, contracted at its opening, and divided at the edge into five lance-pointed divisions, which are whole or pinnatifid. The corolla is inserted at the mouth of the tube of the calyx, and is composed of five heart-shaped petals, which constitute the Rose in its single or natural state. The double blossoms are formed by the change of the stamens and pistils into petals or flower leaves, shorter than those of the corolla proper. The fruit or seed vessel, or *hip*, is formed by the tube of the calyx, which becomes plump and juicy, globular or oviform, having but one cell, and containing numerous small, one-seeded, dry fruits, which usually pass for seeds; these are oval or globular, and surrounded with a soft down. The wood is very hard and compact, and of fine grain; and if it could be procured of sufficient size, would serve as a substitute for box in many kinds of manufacture. The longevity of the Rose is, perhaps, greater than that of any other shrub. We recollect seeing a rose-tree near an old castle in Stoke Newington, England, the stem of which was of immense size, and indicated great age. "There is a rose-bush flourishing at the residence of A. Murray McIlvaine, near Bristol, (Penn.,) known to be more than a hundred years old. In the year 1742, there was a kitchen built, which encroached on the corner of the garden, and the masons laid the corner-stone with great care, saying 'it was a pity to destroy so pretty a bush.' Since then, it has never failed to produce a profusion of roses, shedding around the most delicious of all perfumes. Sometimes it has climbed for years over the second-story windows, and then declined by degrees to the ordinary height. The fifth generation is now regaled with its sweets."

The number of species known to the ancients was small, compared with the number now recognized by botanists. Pliny, with whom we find the most detail on this point, says that the most esteemed were those of Præneste and Pæstum, which were, perhaps, identical; those of Campania and Malta, of a bright red color, and having but twelve petals; the white roses of Heraclea, in Greece, and those of Alabande, which seem to be identical with *R. centifolia.* According to the Roman naturalist and to Theophrastus, they grew naturally on Mount Panga, and produced there very small flowers; yet the inhabitants of Philippi went there to obtain them, and the bushes on being transplanted, produced much improved and beautiful roses. Pliny speaks also of some other species, one whose flowers were single, another which he terms *Spinola*, and also that of Carthage, which bloomed in winter. Unfortunately, all that we find in his works on this subject is, generally, very obscure, and it is difficult to compare many he has described with those known at the present day.

Although there are no double wild roses known at the present day, either in Europe or in this country, yet, as other flowers have been found double in a wild state, it is not impossible that some of the ancient varieties bore double flowers in their native condition in the fields. Such may have been the *Centifolias*, mentioned by Pliny and Theophrastus, as growing upon Mount Panga, and those which, at a still earlier period, according to Herodotus, grew wild in Macedonia, near the ancient gardens of Midas.

The poverty in description which we have observed in ancient writings, and their comparatively small number of species, extends also to a much later day. In a little treatise published in France in 1536, and entitled *De re Hortensis Libellus*, there are but four species mentioned, and scarcely anything concerning their culture. An Italian work published in 1563 mentions only eight species. In the *Florilegium* of Sweet, a folio volume printed at Frankfort in 1612, are ten very coarse representations of roses, but with no indication of their names.

In the *Paradisus Terrestris* of Parkinson, a folio volume printed at London in 1629, some twenty-four kinds are mentioned. Some of them are represented by figures in wood, which are very coarse, and scarcely allow recognition of their species. In the *Jardinier Hollandois*, printed at Amsterdam in 1669, are found but fourteen species of roses, very vaguely described, with scarcely anything on culture.

The first work which treated of roses with any degree of method is that of La Quintyne, published at Paris in 1690, and yet its details of the different species and varieties do not occupy more than a page and a half, while twenty-one pages are given to the culture of tulips, and fifty to pinks. Though he describes two hundred and twenty-five varieties of pinks, and four hundred and thirteen tulips, he mentions only fourteen species and varieties of roses. For a century subsequent to the publication of La Quintyne's work, the Rose is very little mentioned, either in English or French works, and there is nothing to indicate the existence at that time of many species, two or three only being required for medicine and perfumery. Some of the English collections, however, numbered during that century some twenty-two distinct species, and a number of varieties. In 1762, Linnæus was acquainted with only fourteen species. In 1799, Wildenow, in his *Species Plantarum*, mentioned thirty-nine; and Persoon, a little later, reached forty-five species; De Candolle, in his *Prodromus*, published in 1825, increased the number to one hundred and forty-six; and Don, in 1832, makes two hundred and five species. If to these are added those which have been within fifteen years discovered in the Himalaya Mountains, and in other parts of the globe, the number will be greatly increased.

Many of those enumerated by Don should not, in truth, be considered distinct species, and quite a number are nothing more than varieties. In fact, roses are so liable to pass into each other, that botanists are now of the opinion that limits between many of those called species do not exist; a fact which was strongly suspected by Linnæus, when he said, "Species limitibus difficillime circumscribuntur, et forte natura non eos posuit."

There is much confusion in the genus Rosa, and in the best arrangement there may be many, which, on close examination, would scarcely deserve the name of species. The best scientific work on the Rose is the "Monographia Rosarum," by Dr. Lindley. This author, and Loudon, we shall follow entirely in our botanical classification. The latter enumerates several other works on the Rose, which are not within our reach.

The Rose is found in almost every part of the northern hemisphere, between the 19th and 70th degrees of latitude.

Captain Fremont, (now General Fremont) in his description of the prairies some five hundred miles west of St. Louis, says, "Everywhere the Rose is met with, and reminds us of cultivated gardens and civilization. It is scattered over the prairies in small bouquets, and, when glittering in the dews and waving in the pleasant breeze of the early morning, is the most beautiful of the prairie flowers."

It is found from the mountains of Mexico to Hudson's Bay, from the coast of Barbary to Sweden, in Lapland and Siberia, from Spain to the Indies, China, and Kamschatka. "In Asia, half the species have been found; of the thirty-nine which it produces, eighteen are natives of the Russian dominions and the countries adjacent. Most of these are very similar to the European portion of the genus, and five are common to both Europe and Asia. Of the remainder, one, which is, perhaps, a distinct genus, has been discovered in Persia, fifteen in China, and two of the latter, with four others, in the north of India.

We shall not here describe all the species mentioned by Lindley and Loudon; but only those which are the parents of our garden sorts. A large part of the species described by these authors cannot be found in any collection in this country; and, in fact, very few possess any interest except to the botanist. The descriptions here given are mainly abbreviated from those of Loudon.

BRACTEATÆ.—Bracted Roses.

This section is readily distinguished by the woolliness of branches and fruit. Leaves dense, usually shining;

prickles placed under the stipules in pairs. Sepals simple, or nearly so.

R. bracteata, *Wendl.*—THE LARGE-BRACTED ROSE.—Macartney Rose. Evergreen. Branches upright. Prickles stout, recurved, in many instances in pairs. Leaflets 5—9, obovate, subserrate, coriaceous, glossy, glabrous. Stipules scarcely attached to the petiole, bristle-shaped, but fringed. Peduncles and calyxes tomentose. Flowers showy, pure white, solitary, nearly sessile. Fruit spherical, orange red. Native of China; growing to the height of five feet or six feet, and flowering from June to October.

A very ornamental shrub, evergreen, with large white flowers, and numerous bright yellow stamens and styles. It flowers abundantly, but is rather tender in England. It succeeds best when trained against a wall.

R. microphylla, *Roxb.*—THE SMALL-LEAFLETED ROSE.—Hoi-tong-hong, *Chinese.* Stem almost without prickles. Leaflets glossy, sharply serrated, veiny beneath, with densely netted, anastomosing veins. Stipules very narrow, unequal. Calyx densely invested with prickles. Sepals short, broadly ovate, bristly, ending in a point. Prickles having at the base two longitudinal furrows. Flowers very large, double, and of a delicate blush color. Native of China; growing to the height of two feet or three feet, and flowering from August to October.

PIMPINELLIFOLIÆ. LINDL.

Plants bearing crowded, nearly equal, prickles, or unarmed. Bractless, rarely bracteate. Leaflets ovate or oblong. Sepals connivent, permanent. Disk almost wanting.

This section is essentially different from the last in habit, but in artificial characters they approach very nearly. It, however, may be distinguished by the great number of leaflets, which vary from seven to thirteen, and even to fifteen, instead of from five to seven. The flowers are also without bracts, except in some species not mentioned here. These, having connivent permanent sepals, cannot be confounded with the preceding division; nor, on account of their disk, with the following. There is no instance of stipular prickles in the present tribe. The sepals are entire, or nearly so.

R. sulphurea, *Ait.*—THE SULPHUR-COLORED ROSE.—The Double Yellow Rose. *Synonyms.* R. hemispherica, *Herm.* R. glaucophylla, *Ehrh.* Rosa lutea flore pleno, *Rai. Hist.* R. lutea, *Brot.* Stipules linear, divaricate, dilated at the apex. Leaflets glaucous, flattish. Tube hemispherical. Stem prickles unequal, scattered. Flowers large, of a fine transparent yellow, always double. Native of the Levant; growing to the height of from four feet to ten feet, and flowering in July.

This sort does not flower freely, except in open, airy situations and trained against a wall, exposed to the north or east, rather than to the south. Its flower buds are apt to burst on one side before they expand, and, consequently, to become deformed; to prevent this, the blossom buds should be thinned, and care taken that they have abundance of light and air. Watering it freely in the flowering season is also found advantageous, and the shoots in general ought not to be shortened. This beautiful species is said to flower freely, if grafted on the musk cluster at eight feet or ten feet from the ground; or it will do well on the China rose. It is grown in great abundance in Italy, where its flowers produce a magnificent effect, from their large size, doubleness, and brilliant yellow color. It is one of the oldest inhabitants of our gardens, though the exact year of its introduction is unknown. "Ludovico Berthema tells us, in 1503, that he saw great quantities of yellow roses at Calicut, whence it appears probable that both the single and double-flowered varieties were brought into Europe by the Turks; as Parkinson tells us, in a work which he dedicated to Henrietta, the queen of our unfortunate Charles I., that the double yellow rose 'was first procured to be brought to England by Master Nicholas Lete, a worthy merchant of London, and a great lover of flowers, from Constantinople, which (as we hear) was first brought thither from Syria, but perished quickly, both with him, and with all others to whom he imparted it; yet afterward it was sent to Master John de Franqueville, a merchant of London, and a great lover of all rose plants, as well as flowers, from which is sprung the greatest store that is now flourishing in this kingdom.'"

R. spinosissima, *L.*—The Most Spiny, or Scotch Rose. —Prickles unequal. Leaflets flat, glabrous, simply serrated. A dwarf, compact bush, with creeping suckers. Flowers small, solitary, white or blush-colored. Fruit ovate, or nearly round, black or dark purple. Native of Europe; plentiful in Britain. Shrub, one foot to two feet high; flowering in May and June.

Varieties. A great many varieties of this rose have been raised, with flowers double, semi-double, white, purple, red, and even yellow. The first double variety was found in a wild state, in the neighborhood of Perth.

CENTIFOLIÆ.—Hundred-leaved Roses.

Shrubs, all bearing bristles and prickles. Peduncles bracteate. Leaflets oblong or ovate, wrinkled. Disk thickened, closing the throat. Sepals compound. This division comprises the portion of the genus *Rosa* which has most particularly interested the lover of flowers. It is probable that the earliest roses of which there are any records of being cultivated, belonged to this section; but to which particular species those of Cyrene or Mount Panga are to be referred, it is now too late to inquire. The attar of Roses, which is an important article of commerce, is either obtained from roses belonging to this division indiscriminately, as in the manufactory at Florence, conducted by a convent of friars; or from some particular kind, as in India. It appears, from specimens brought from Chizapore by Colonel Hardwicke, that *R. Damascena* is there exclusively used for obtaining the essential oil. The Persians also make use of a sort which Kæmpfer calls *R. Shirazensis*, (from its growing about Shiraz), in preference to others; this may be either *R. Damascena R. Gallica*, or *R. centifolia*, or, perhaps, *R. moschata*. The species contained in the present section are all setigerous, by which they are distinguished from the following divisions; their thickened disk and divided sepals separate them from the preceding. To the section of Rubiginosæ the glanduliferous sorts approach; but the difference of their glands, the size of their flowers, and their dissimilar habit, prevent their being confounded.

R. Damascena.—THE DAMASCUS, OR DAMASK ROSE.—Rose à quatre Saisons. *Synonyms.* R. Belgica, *Mill.* R. calendarum, *Munch.* R. bifera, *Poir.* Prickles unequal, the large ones falcate. Sepals reflexed. Fruit elongated. Native of Syria. Flowers large, white or red, single or double. The present species may be distinguished from *R. centifolia* by the greater size of the prickles, the greenness of the bark, the elongated fruit, and the long, reflexed sepals. The petals of this species, and all the varieties of *R. centifolia*, as well as those of other species, are employed indiscriminately for the purpose of making rose-water. A shrub, growing from two feet to eight feet high, and flowering in June and July

This species is extremely beautiful, from the size and brilliant color of its flowers. It is asserted by some writers to have been brought from Damascus in Syria at the time of the Crusades, but there is every probability that it came from Italy, since it is the same as the *Bifera*, or the twice-bearing rose of the ancient Roman gardeners, and is the original type of our Remontant Roses. The Roman gardeners could have produced a certain autumnal bloom only by a sort of retarding process; for, although the Damask Rose will, under peculiar circumstances, bloom in autumn of its own accord, yet it cannot always be relied upon to do so. During the early period of the French monarchy, when none of the Remontant Roses were known, and this species was common, it was considered quite a phenomenon to see them appear naturally in winter. Gregory, of Tours, speaking of the year 584, says, "This year many prodigies appeared, and many calamities afflicted the people, for roses were seen blooming in January, and a circle was formed around the sun." And of the year 589 he says, "This year trees blossomed in autumn, and bore fruit the second time, and roses appeared in the ninth month."

R. centifolia, *Lin.*—THE HUNDRED-PETALED, PROVENCE, OR CABBAGE ROSE.—*Synonyms.* R. provincialis, *Mill.* R. polyanthos, *Rossig.* R. caryophyllea, *Poir.* R. unguiculata, *Desf.* R. varians, *Pohl.* Prickles unequal, the larger ones falcate. Leaflets ciliated with glands. Flowers drooping. Calyxes clammy. Fruit oblong. Native of Eastern Caucasus, in groves. Flowers white or red; single, but most commonly double.

This species is distinguished from *R. Damascena* by the sepals not being reflexed, and the flowers having their petals curved inwards, so as, in the double state, to give the flower the appearance of the heart of a cabbage, whence the name of the Cabbage Rose. Its fruit is either oblong or roundish, but never elongated. From *R. Gallica* it is distinguished by the flowers being drooping, and by the larger size of the prickles, with a more robust habit. A shrub, growing from three feet to six feet high, and flowering in June and July. When this rose becomes unthrifty from age, it is renewed by cutting off the stems close to the ground as soon as the flowers have fallen; shoots will then be produced, sufficiently vigorous to furnish a beautiful and abundant bloom the following spring.

Varieties. Above one hundred varieties have been assigned to this species, and classed in three divisions:

Var. **provincialis** includes the Provence, or Cabbage Roses.

Var. **muscosa** comprises the Moss Roses.

Var. **pomponia,** the Pompone Roses. According to Loudon, we have made this a variety of *R. centifôlia,* although some authors assert it to have been found growing wild in 1735, by a gardener of Dijon, in France, who discovered it while cutting wood on a mountain near that city. Many varieties of it have been obtained, among which, the most singular is the little dwarf given in the New Du Hamel as a distinct species. It does not grow more than twelve or fifteen inches high, and frequently perishes before blossoming.

Var. **bipinnata,** *Red,* has bipinnate leaves.

R. Gallica, *L.*—THE FRENCH, OR PROVENCE ROSE. RED ROSE.—*Synonyms.* R. centifolia, *Mill.* R. sylvatica, *Gater.* R. rubra, *Lam.* R. holosericea, *Rossig.* R. Belgica, *Brot.* R. blanda, *Brot.* Prickles unequal. Stipules narrow, divaricate at the tip. Leaflets, 5—7, coriaceous, rigid, ovate or lanceolate, deflexed. Flower bud ovate-globose; Sepals spreading during the time of the flowering. Fruit, subglobose, very coriaceous. Calyx and peduncle more or less hispid with glanded hairs, somewhat viscose.

A species allied to *R. centifolia, L.*, but with round fruit, and very coriaceous leaflets, with more numerous nerves, that are a little prominent, and are anastomosing. Native of middle Europe and Caucasus, in hedges. The flowers vary from red to crimson, and from single to double; and there is one variety with the flowers double white. The petals of some of the varieties of this rose are used in medicine, which, though not so fragrant as those of the Dutch hundred-leaved rose, also one of the varieties of this species, are preferred for their beautiful color and their pleasant astringency. The petals of *R. Gallica* are those which are principally used for making conserve of roses, and, when dried, for gargles: their odor is increased by drying. They are also used in common with those of *R. centifolia*, for making rose-water and attar of roses. This rose was called by old writers the Red Rose, and is supposed to have been the one assumed as the badge of the House of Lancaster. This, also, is one of the roses mentioned by Pliny; from which, he says, all the others have been derived. It is often confounded with the Damask rose.

Varieties. The varieties of this species are very numerous. One of the most distinct is Var. **parvifolia.** (R. parvifolia, *Ehr.* R. Burgundiaca, *Rossig.* R. remensis, *Desf.*) THE BURGUNDY ROSE.—A dwarf, compact shrub, with stiff, ovate acute, and sharply serrated small leaflets, and very double purple flowers, which are solitary, and have some resemblance, in form and general appearance, to the flower of a double-flowered Asiatic Ranunculus.

VILLOSÆ.—HAIRY ROSES.

Suckers erect. Prickles straightish. Leaflets ovate or oblong, with diverging serratures. Sepals connivent, permanent. Disk thickened, closing the throat. This division borders equally close upon those of Caninæ and Rubiginosæ. From both it is distinguished by its root-suckers being erect and stout. The most absolute marks of difference, however, between this and Caninæ, exist in the prickles of the present section being straight, and the serratures of the leaves diverging. If, as is sometimes the case, the prickles of this tribe are falcate, the serratures become more diverging. The permanent sepals are another character by which this tribe may be known from Caninæ. Rubiginosæ cannot be confounded with the present section, on account of the unequal hooked prickles and glandular leaves of the species. Roughness of fruit and permanence of sepals are common to both.

R. alba, *Lin.*—The Common White Rose.—Leaflets oblong, glaucous, rather naked above, simply serrated. Prickles straightish or falcate, slender or strong, without bristles. Sepals pinnate, reflexed. Fruit unarmed. Native of Piedmont, Cochin China, Denmark, France, and Saxony. Flowers large, either white, or of the most delicate blush color, with a grateful fragrance. Fruit oblong, scarlet, or blood-colored. A shrub, growing from four feet to ten feet in height, and flowering in June and July.

RUBIGINOSÆ.—Brier Roses.

Prickles unequal, sometimes bristle-formed, rarely wanting. Leaflets ovate or oblong, glandular, with diverging serratures. Sepals permanent. Disk thickened. Root-shoots arched. The numerous glands on the lower surface of the leaves will be sufficient to prevent anything else being referred to this section; and although *R. tomentosa* has sometimes glandular leaves, the inequality of the prickles of the species of Rubiginosæ, and their red fruit, will clearly distinguish them. This division includes all the Eglantine, or Sweet-brier Roses.

R. rubiginosa *Lin.*—Rusty-leaved Rose, Sweet-Brier, or Eglantine.—R. suavifolia, *Lightf.* R. Eglanteria, *Mill.* R. agrestis, *Savi.* R. rubiginosa parviflora, *Rau.* Prickles hooked, compressed, with smaller straighter ones interspersed. Leaflets elliptical, doubly serrated, hairy, clothed beneath with rust-colored glands. Sepals pinnate, and bristly, as well as the peduncles. Fruit obovate, bristly toward the base. Native throughout Europe, and of Caucasus. In Britain, in bushy places, on a dry gravelly or chalky soil. Leaves sweet-scented when bruised, and resembling the fragrance of the Pippin Apple. When dried in the shade, and prepared as a tea, they make a healthful and pleasant beverage.

This species is extensively used in Europe for the formation of Tea Roses, and it is estimated that two hundred thousand are budded annually in the vicinity of

Paris alone. The species is very vigorous, but does not seem to answer well in our hot sun. The change from its native shaded thickets and hedges is too much for its tall, exposed stem, and, although the stock may not itself die, yet the variety budded upon it will frequently perish in two or three years. This is doubtless partly owing to a want of analogy between the stock and the variety given it for nourishment, but that the former is the prominent evil is evident by the fact that dwarfs of the same stock, where the stem is shaded by the foliage, flourish much better. The Eglantine, in favored situations, is very long-lived. A French writer speaks of one in which he had counted one hundred and twenty concentric layers, thus making its age the same number of years. Another writer speaks of an Eglantine in Lower Saxony, whose trunk separated into two very strong branches, twenty-four feet high, and extending over a space of twenty feet. At the height of seven feet, one of the branches is nearly six inches, and the other four inches, in circumference. There is a tradition that it existed in the time of Louis the Pious, King of Germany in the ninth century. This, however, must evidently be received with some allowance. Flowers, pink. Fruit, scarlet, obovate or elliptic. A shrub, growing from four feet to six feet in height, and flowering in June and July.

CANINÆ.—Dog Roses.

Prickles equal, hooked. Leaflets ovate, glandless or glandular, with the serratures conniving. Sepals deciduous. Disk thickened, closing the throat. Larger suckers arched.

R. canina, *Lin.*—Dog Rose.—*Synonyms.* R. glauca, *Lois.* R. arvensis, *Schrank.* R. glaucescens, *Mer.* R. nitens, *Mer.* R. teneriffensis, *Donn.* R. senticosa, *Achar.*

Prickles strong, hooked. Leaflets simply serrated, pointed, quite smooth. Sepals pinnate. Fruit ovate, smooth, or rather bristly, like the aggregate flower stalks. Native throughout Europe, and the north of Africa; plentiful in Britain, in hedges, woods, and thickets. Flowers rather large, pale red, seldom white. Fruit, ovate, bright scarlet, of a peculiar and very grateful flavor, especially if made into a conserve with sugar. The pulp of the fruit, besides saccharine matter, contains citric acid, which gives it an acid taste. The pulp, before it is used, should be carefully cleared from the nuts or seeds. A shrub, growing to the height of six feet or ten feet, and flowering in June and July.

R. Indica, *L.*—THE INDIA OR CHINA ROSE.—Stem upright, whitish, or green, or purple. Prickles stout, falcate, distant. Leaflets 3 to 5, ovate-acuminate, coriaceous, shining, glabrous, serrulate, the surfaces of different colors. Stipules very narrow, connate with the petiole, almost entire, or serrate. Flowers solitary, or in panicles. Stamens bent inward. Peduncle sub-articulate, mostly thickened upward, and with the calyx smooth, or wrinkled and bristly. Native of China, near Canton. Flowers red, usually semi-double. Petioles setigerous and prickly. Petals obcordate. A shrub, growing to the height of from 4 feet to 20 feet, and flowering throughout the year.

Varieties.—There are numerous varieties of this beautiful rose in cultivation, some of which were regarded as distinct species by the earlier authors. The following are quite distinct, and may each be considered the type of a long list of subvarieties.

Var. Noisettiana.—THE NOISETTE ROSE.—Stem firm, and, as well as the branches, prickly. Stipules nearly entire. Flowers panicled, very numerous, semi-double, pale red. Styles exserted.

This well-known and very beautiful rose is almost invaluable in a shrubbery, from its free and vigorous growth, and the profusion of its flowers, which are continually being produced during the whole summer.

Var. odoratissima.—THE TEA-SCENTED CHINA ROSE.

—R. odoratissima, *Swt.;* R. Indica fragrans, *Red.*—Has semi-double flowers, of a most delicious fragrance, strongly resembling the scent of the finest green tea. There are numerous subvarieties.

R. Laurenciana is placed as a species by some authors, but it is probably only a variety of *R. Indica.*

SYSTYLÆ.

(From *sun*, together, and *stulos*, a style; in reference to the styles being connected.)

Sect. Char.—Styles cohering together into an elongated column. Stipules adnate. The habit of this section is nearly the same as that of the last. The leaves are frequently persistent.

R. sempervirens, *Lin.* — EVERGREEN ROSE. — *Syn.* R. scandens, *Mill.;* R. Balearica, *Desf.;* R. atrovirens, *Viv.;* R. sempervirens globosa, *Red.*—Evergreen. Shoots climbing. Prickles pretty equal, falcate. Leaves of 5 to 7 leaflets, that are green on both sides, coriaceous. Flowers almost solitary, or in corymbs. Sepals nearly entire, longish. Styles cohering into an elongate pilose column. Fruit ovate or ovate-globose, orange-colored. Peduncles mostly hispid with glanded hairs. Closely allied to *R. arvensis*, but differing in its being evergreen, in its leaves being coriaceous, and in its stipules being subfalcate, and more acute at the tip. Native of France, Portugal, Italy, Greece, and the Balearic Islands. A climbing shrub, flowering from June to August.

Used for the same purposes as the Ayrshire Rose, from which it differs in retaining its leaves the greater part of the winter, and in its less vigorous shoots. This species is well adapted for *rose carpets* made by pegging down its long, flexile shoots. Its glossy, rich foliage forms, in this way, a beautiful carpet of verdure enameled with flowers.

R. multiflora, *Thunb.*—MANY-FLOWERED ROSE.—*Syn.* R. flava, *Donn.;* R. florida, *Poir.;* R. diffusa, *Roxb.*—Branches, peduncles, and calyxes tomentose. Shoots very long. Prickles slender, scattered. Leaflets 5 to 7, ovate-lanceolate, soft, finely wrinkled. Stipules pectinate. Flowers in corymbs, and, in many instances, very numerous. Buds ovate globose. Sepals short. Styles protruded, incompletely grown together into a long, hairy column. A climbing shrub, a native of Japan and China; and producing a profusion of clustered heads of single, semi-double, or double, white, pale red, or red flowers in June and July.

This is one of the most ornamental of climbing roses; but, to succeed, even in the climate of London, it requires a wall. The flowers continue to expand one after another during nearly two months.

Var. Grevillei.—R. Roxburghii, *Hort.;* R. platyphylla, *Red.* — THE SEVEN SISTERS ROSE.—A beautiful variety, with much larger and more double flowers than the species, of a purplish color. It is easily known from *R. multiflora* by the fringed edge of the stipules; while those of the common *R. multiflora* have much less fringe, and the leaves are smaller, with the leaflets much less rugose. The form of the blossoms and corymbs is pretty nearly the same in both.

A plant of this variety on the gable end of R. Donald's house, in the Goldworth Nursery, in England, in 1826, covered above 100 square feet, and had more than 100 corymbs of bloom. Some of the corymbs had more than 50 buds in a cluster, and the whole averaged about 30 in each corymb, so that the amount of flower buds was about 3,000. The variety of color produced by the buds at first opening was not less astonishing than their number. White, light blush, deeper blush, light red, darker red, scarlet, and purple flowers, all appeared in the same corymb; and the production of these seven colors at once is said to be the reason why this plant is called the Seven Sisters Rose. This tree produced a shoot the same year which grew 18 feet in length in two or three weeks. This variety, when in a deep, free soil, and an airy situation, is of very vigorous growth, and a free flowerer; but the shoots are of a bramble-like texture, and the plant, in consequence, is of but temporary duration. R. Donald's *R. Grevillei* died in three or four years.

Var. Russelliana is a variety differing considerably, in flowers and foliage, from the species, but retaining the fringed footstalk; and is, hence, quite distinct from *R. sempervirens Russelliana.*

Var. Boursaulti, BOURSAULT ROSE, is placed, in Don's *Miller*, under this species; though it differs more from the preceding variety than many species do from each other. It is comparatively a hard-wooded, durable rose, and valuable for flowering early and freely. This is a very remarkable rose, from its petals having a reticulated appearance.

R. moschata, *Mill.*—MUSK ROSE.—*Syn.* R. glandulifera, *Roxb.*—Shoots ascending. Prickles upon the stem slender, recurved. Leaflets 5 to 7, lanceolate, acuminate, nearly glabrous, the two surfaces of different colors. Stipules very narrow, acute. Flowers, in many instances, very numerous, white, with the claws of the petals yellow, very fragrant. Lateral peduncles jointed, and, as well as the calyx, pilose, and almost hispid. Sepals almost pinnately cut, long. Fruit red, ? ovate.

The branches of the Musk Rose are generally too weak to support, without props, its large bunches of flowers, which are produced in an umbel-like manner at their extremities. The musky odor is very perceptible, even at some distance from the plant, particularly in the evening,—

> "When each inconstant breeze that blows
> Steals essence from the musky rose."

It is said to be a native of Barbary; but this has been doubted. It is, however, found wild in Tunis, and is cultivated there for the sake of an essential oil, which is obtained from the petals by distillation. It has also been found wild in Spain. The first record of the musk rose having been cultivated in England is in *Hakluyt*, in 1582, who states that the musk rose was brought to England from Italy. It was in common cultivation in the time of

Gerard, and was formerly much valued for its musky fragrance, when that scent was the fashionable perfume. The Persian attar of roses is said to be obtained from this species. The musk rose does best trained against a wall, on account of the length and weakness of its branches; and Miller adds that it should always be pruned in spring, as in winter it will not bear the knife. It requires very little pruning, as the flowers are produced at the extremities of the shoots, which are often 10 feet or 12 feet in length. It flowers freely, and is well worthy of cultivation. This rose is thought by some to be the same as that of Cyrene, which Athenæus has mentioned as affording a delicious perfume, but of this there is no certain evidence. It seems to have been rare in Europe in the time of Gessner, the botanist, who, in a letter to Dr. Occon, dated Zurich, 1565, says that it was growing in a garden at Augsburg, and he was extremely anxious that the doctor should procure some of its shoots for him. Rivers mentions that Olivier, a French traveler, speaks of a rose tree at Ispahan, called the "Chinese Rose Tree," fifteen feet high, formed by the union of several stems, each four or five inches in diameter. Seeds of this tree were sent to Paris and produced the common Musk Rose.

BANKSIANÆ.—Banksia Roses.

(So called because all the species contained in this section agree in character with *R. Banksiæ*, a rose named in honor of Lady Banks.)

Stipules nearly free, subulate, or very narrow, usually deciduous. Leaflets usually ternate, shining. Stems climbing. The species of this section are remarkable for their long, graceful, and often climbing, shoots, drooping flowers, and trifoliate, shining leaves. They are particularly distinguished by their deciduous, subulate, or very narrow stipules. Their fruit is very variable.

R. Banksiæ, *R. Br.*—Lady Banks' or Banksia Rose. —Without prickles, glabrous, smooth. Leaflets 3 to 5, lanceolate, sparingly serrated, approximate. Stipules bristle-like, scarcely attached to the petiole, rather glossy, deciduous. Flowers in umbel-like corymbs, numerous, very double, sweet-scented, nodding. Tube of the calyx a little dilated at the tip. Fruit globose, black. A native of China. A climbing shrub, flowering in June and July.

Description, etc.—This is an exceedingly beautiful and very remarkable kind of rose; the flowers being small, round, and very double, on long peduncles, and resembling in form the flowers of the double French cherry, or that of a small ranunculus, more than those of the generality of roses. The flowers of *R. Banksiæ alba* are remarkably fragrant, the scent strongly resembling that of violets.

Thunberg speaks of the *Rosa rugosa* as growing in China and Japan, being extensively cultivated in the gardens of those countries, and producing flowers of a pale red or pure white. The original plant is of a deep purple color. Siebold, in his treatise on the flowers of Japan, says that this rose had been already cultivated in China about eleven hundred years, and that the ladies of the Court, under the dynasty of Long, prepared a very choice pot-pourri by mixing its petals with musk and camphor.

More than one hundred distinct species are mentioned by botanists, in addition to those we have enumerated, but none of very marked characters or much known.

CHAPTER II.

GARDEN CLASSIFICATION.

The varieties of a plant are, by Botanists, designated by names intended to convey an idea of certain characteristics,—the form and consistency of the leaves, the arrangement, number, size, and color of the flowers, seed-vessels, etc. The varieties of roses, however, have so few distinct characteristics, that florists find it difficult to give any name expressive of the very slight shades of difference in the color or form of the flower. Fanciful names have therefore been chosen, indiscriminately, according to the taste of the grower; and we thus find classed, in brotherly nearness, Napoleon and Wellington, Queen Victoria and Louis Philippe, Othello and Wilberforce, with many others. Any half-dozen English or French rose growers may give the name of their favorite Wellington or Napoleon to a rose raised by each of them, and entirely different in form and color from the other five bearing the same name. Thus has arisen the great confusion in rose nomenclature.

A still greater difficulty and confusion, however, exists in the classification adopted by the various English and French rose growers. By these, classes are multiplied and roses placed in them without sufficient attention to their distinctive characters; these are subsequently changed to other classes, to the utter confusion of those who are really desirous of obtaining some knowledge of the respective varieties. Even Rivers, the most correct of them all, has in several catalogues the same rose in as many different classes, and his book may perhaps place it in another. He thus comments upon this constant change:

"Within the last ten years, how many plants have been named and unnamed, classed and re-classed!—Professor A. placing it here, and Dr. B. placing it there! I can almost imagine Dame Nature laughing in her sleeve, when our philosophers are thus puzzled. Well, so it is, in a measure, with roses; a variety has often equal claims to two classes. First impressions have perhaps placed it in one, and there rival amateurs should let it remain."

If there exists, then, this doubt of the proper class to which many roses belong, we think it would be better to drop entirely this sub-classification, and adopt some more general heads, under one of which every rose *can* be classed. It may often be difficult to ascertain whether a rose is a Damask, a Provence, or a Hybrid China; but there can be no difficulty in ascertaining whether it is dwarf or climbing, whether it blooms once or more in the year, and whether the leaves are rough as in the Remontants, or smooth as in the Bengals. We have therefore endeavored to simplify the old classification, and have placed all roses under three principal heads, viz:

I. Those that make distinct and separate periods of bloom throughout the season, as the Remontant Roses.

II. Those that bloom continually, without any temporary cessation, as the Bourbon, China, etc.

III. Those that bloom only once in the season, as the French and others.

Remontants.—The first of these divisions includes only the present Damask and Hybrid Perpetuals, and for these we know no term so expressive as the French *Remontant.* "*Perpetual*" does not express their true character.

Everblooming Roses is the name we give to those included under the second general head. This is divided into five classes:

1. The **Bourbon,** the varieties of which are easily known by their luxuriant growth, and thick, large, leathery leaves. These are, moreover, reasonably hardy.

2. The **China.**—This includes the present China, Tea, and Noisette Roses, which are now much confused, as there are many among the Teas which are not tea-scented, and among the Noisettes are those which do not bloom in clusters; they are, moreover, so much alike in their growth and habit, that it is better each should stand upon its own merits, and not on the characteristics of an imaginary class.

3. **Musk.**—Roses of this class are known by their rather rougher foliage.

4. **Macartney.**—The varieties of this are distinguished by their very rich, glossy, almost evergreen foliage.

5. **Microphylla.**—A class easily distinguished by their peculiar foliage and straggling habit.

The third general head we divide again into five classes:

1. **Garden Roses.**—This includes all the present French, Provence, Hybrid Provence, Hybrid China, Hybrid Bourbon, White, and Damask Roses, many of which, under the old arrangement, differ more from others in their own class than from many in another class.

2. **Moss Roses,** all of which are easily distinguished.

3. **Brier Roses,** which will include the Sweet-Brier, Hybrid Sweet-Brier, and Austrian Brier.

4. **Scotch Roses.**

5. **Climbing Roses;** which are again divided into all the distinctive subdivisions.

In describing colors, we have given those which prevail. It is well known that many roses are very variable in this respect, and that the same flower will frequently be white or yellow, crimson or blush, at different periods of its bloom. We have seen a plant produce several flowers totally unlike each other; one being dark crimson, and the other pale blush. We therefore describe the *prevailing* color, and the cultivator should not be disappointed if his rose, the first season, should not correspond with the description; neither should he be disappointed if a rose which we describe as very double should with him prove very single. Transplanting will often temporarily change the character of roses, and they often refuse to develop themselves perfectly under our hot sun, or in a poor soil. A second season is thus often required to test them fairly. We have seen the fine rose, La Reine, semi-double, and worthless at midsummer, while at other seasons, and perhaps in a different location, it is fully equal to its reputation. It is frequently the case, that roses imported from Europe, under glowing descriptions, prove worthless the first season, but fully sustain their character the second. We mention these things here, in order that the amateur may be prepared for any temporary disappointment that may occur. In describing over two hundred choice varieties, we have endeavored to select those whose character is well established for superior and distinct qualities, and above all, for vigorous growth. Any variety whose growth is uniformly weak has been at once rejected, notwithstanding its great beauty of flower. Thus many fine roses, like Gloire de Santenay, are thrown aside. There are many equally good that have been necessarily omitted, and there are also new varieties we have recently received from Europe, which may prove superior to many we have named.

From this list, the rose amateur may feel safe in selecting, without incurring the risk of obtaining inferior varieties.

ROSES THAT BLOOM DURING THE WHOLE SEASON.

REMONTANT ROSES.

The term Remontant—signifying, literally, *to grow again*—we have chosen to designate this class of roses, there being no word in our own language equally expressive. They were formerly called Damask and Hybrid

Fig. 1.—REMONTANT ROSE.

Perpetuals, but are distinguished from the true Perpetual or Everblooming Roses by their peculiarity of distinct and separate periods of bloom. They bloom with the other roses in early summer, then cease for a while, then make a fresh season of bloom, and thus through the summer and autumn, differing entirely from the Bourbon and Bengal Roses, which grow and bloom continually through the summer. In order, therefore, to avoid confusion, we have deemed it best to adopt the French term, *Remontant.*

These roses have generally been obtained by hybridization between the Hybrid China and Damask, and the Bourbon and China Roses, uniting the luxuriant growth and hardy character of the former two with the everblooming qualities of the latter. They are generally large, double, very fragrant, and bloom, some of them, freely throughout the season. They are also perfectly hardy, and grow well in any climate without protection. These qualities render them very desirable, and they are fast driving out of cultivation the Garden Roses, which bloom but once, and during the rest of the season cumber the ground. There are, it is true, among the latter, some varieties, like Madame Plantier, Chénédole, Persian Yellow, and others, that are not equaled by any varieties existing among the Remontants. Such, however, is the skill now exerted by rose growers, that this will not long be the case, and we may hope soon to have among the Remontants, roses of every shade of color, with the snow-like whiteness of Madame Plantier, the golden richness of Persian Yellow, or the peculiar brilliancy of Chénédole.

Adam Paul.—A fine grower. Its flower is double, and its color rose, tinged with violet.

Auguste Mie.—A seedling of the well-known La Reine, a vigorous grower. Its color is a light pink, not so dark as La Reine, which it resembles in form.

Ardoise de Lyon.—One of the best of the dark roses; its color is a violet purple.

Achille Goudot.—A striking rose; the upper side of its petals being crimson, and the under side a bright rose color.

Adéle Mauzé.—Of medium size, double, with a light rose color.

Anna Alexieff.—Large and full, with a pink color. Its habit is good, and it is a good variety for forcing. It is one of the most profuse bloomers.

Baronne Prevost.—One of the very best of its class, blooming freely in autumn, and producing fragrant flowers of a bright rose color. It is also of luxuriant growth and large, rich foliage.

Baronne de Maynard.—A vigorous grower, with a well-formed, medium-sized, pure white flower.

Belle Normande.—A good grower, and its color a delicate blush.

Caroline de Sansal.—A vigorous plant, with a large and full flower, the color of which is clear flesh, with blush edges. It is one of the best of its color.

Charles Lefebvre.—A strong grower, and one of the finest of its class. Its color is a bright, changeable crimson, inclining to a purple shade in the centre. Its form is cupped and regular.

Clementine Duval.—Has a dwarf habit, and a bright rose color.

Duchesse de Caylus.—A superb rose, scarcely surpassed by any. Its form is double, and cupped; its color is a rich scarlet crimson.

Duchess of Sutherland.—A plant of luxuriant growth and foliage. Its form is beautifully cupped, and its color a delicate rose. It is, however, not reliable for an autumnal bloom.

Duc de Cazes.—A good grower, and its color is a deep purplish crimson.

Enfant de Mt. Carmel.—A good grower and bloomer. Its color is a dark rose, or crimson.

Elizabeth Vigneron.—A good grower, with rose-colored flowers.

General Jacqueminot.—A strong grower, and when in bud, one of the most beautiful of roses. Its open flower, not being perfectly double, is surpassed by others. Its color is a scarlet crimson, with a soft velvety sheen, and a few thousand of them in full bloom is a sight to be remembered. A basket of buds freshly cut in the morning is sure to be appreciated.

General Washington.—One of the finest of its class. It is a good grower, very full bloomer, and a general favorite. Its color is a bright red.

Giant of Battles.—The most brilliant scarlet Remontant. We describe it here because it is well known for its dazzling color, and in this respect unequaled. It cannot, however, be recommended to any but the most careful grower. In ordinary hands, its growth is weak, and it mildews badly. Under glass, where the mildew can be controlled, it makes a strong and luxuriant growth.

Henry IV.—A well-known rose, of vigorous growth, with a lilac and purplish pink color.

Jacques Lafitte.—A large, vigorous growing, double rose, of a carmine or bright pink color.

Joasine Hanet.—Of medium size, and blooms in clusters. Its color is reddish purple

John Hopper.—Large, and finely shaped. Its color is rosy crimson.

Jules Margottin.—One of the finest Remontant Roses. Its growth is vigorous, its bloom is abundant, and its color is a clear pink crimson. It is particularly fine when in bud.

Kate Hausburg.—One of the most thoroughly remontant, blooming through the summer and autumn. It is very large, and its color is a peculiar light cherry. No collection should be without it.

La Reine.—An old and well-known rose, of the largest size. It is finely cupped, almost globular, very double, and very fragrant. Its color is a bright rose, slightly tinged with lilac. Its foliage and habit are good, and it may fairly rank as one of the best roses. It owes its origin to Laffay, and was sent out in 1843.

Lion des Combats.—A large and full rose, of a reddish violet color, often shaded with scarlet.

Le Géant.—A large crimson-colored rose.

Lord Clyde.—One of the finest of the dark roses, with a deep purplish crimson color.

Louis Van Houtte.—Has a large and double globular flower. Its color is bright shaded rosy carmine.

Mathurin Regnier.—One of the best, with large and full form, and a delicate pale rose color.

Madame Alfred de Rougemont.—A good grower, and autumnal bloomer, and in color nearly white.

Madame Boll.—Very vigorous and hardy, with a full double form, and rose color.

Madame Gustave Bonnett.—One of the best white roses, and blooms freely through the summer.

Madame Louise Carique.—One of the most valuable Remontants. Its color is a fine rosy carmine, its form is full, and it grows well and blooms abundantly through the summer. For general purposes, it has scarcely a superior.

Madame Morand.—Rosy lilac in color, and well cupped in form.

Madame Trotter.—A very strong grower, a most abundant bloomer, with flowers of a deep cherry red. It is shy of blooming in autumn, but the beautiful deep red of its new shoots makes it desirable for every collection.

Maurice Bernardin.—A good grower, with full, fine form, and bright cherry crimson color. It is one of the best.

Pœnee.—Has a unique flower. Its color is rose, veined with scarlet.

Palais de Cristal.—Has a bright flesh color, with a salmon tint.

Pius IX.—A vigorous grower, and abundant bloomer. Its color is crimson, passing into violet.

Prince Camille de Rohan.—Large and full. Its color is a velvety deep crimson maroon, clouded with red. One of the finest.

Reine des Violettes.—A full and distinct flower. Its color is violet purple, with red centre. It is one of the best dark roses.

Reynolds Hole.—One of the finest new Remontants, and is scarcely surpassed by any. It is a good grower, and its color is cherry rose, shaded to white at the base of the petals.

Souvenir de Lady Eardley.—An abundant blooming rose, of a brilliant crimson color.

Souvenir de la Reine d'Angleterre.—One of the largest roses, but requires good culture to open fully. Its color is a clear bright rose.

Sydonie.—Has a fine form, with a clear, light pink color, and is one of the best old roses.

Triomphe d'Amiens.—A fragrant rose, and its color a fine velvety lake, striped with reddish brown.

Victor Trouillard.—Large and full. Its color a brilliant crimson and purple, shaded.

Yolande d'Arragon.—A vigorous grower, with distinct foliage. Its flower is large, and rose-colored.

REMONTANT SCOTCH.

Stanwell.—Of Scotch parentage, and has the peculiar foliage and habit of the Scotch roses. Its flowers are large, blush-colored, and rather flat. It is an abundant and constant bloomer throughout the season, and its peculiar, delightful fragrance renders it very desirable.

REMONTANT MOSS.

These few roses have been separated from the summer-blooming moss roses, because they show a disposition to bloom in the autumn.

Eugene de Savoie.—Of vigorous growth, with a large and full flower. It is an abundant bloomer, and very fragrant. Its color is a bright red.

Madame Edouard Ory.—A good autumn bloomer. It is globular, finely formed, and of a rich rose color.

Perpetual White.—A vigorous grower, double, and blooms in clusters. One of the most desirable.

Raphael.—Of medium size, double, and has a delicate rosy flesh color.

Salet.—A good autumnal bloomer, and a good grower. Its color is bright pink, changing to rose.

BOURBON ROSES.

This class does not possess the hardiness of the Remontants, nor the free blooming properties of the Bengals, Teas, and Noisettes, and therefore can never compete with the former for the North, nor with the latter for the South. In it, however, are varieties like Hermosa, Souvenir de Malmaison, and others, which are scarcely surpassed in any class. The Bourbon Rose has also qualities which make many varieties favorites. These qualities are its greater hardiness than the Tea Rose, its very thick, leathery foliage, its luxuriant growth, its more constant bloom than the Remontants, and its thick, velvety petals, of a consistency to endure the summer's sun.

It was introduced into France by Jacques, head garden-

Fig. 2.—BOURBON ROSE.

er of the Duke of Orleans, at Neuilly, who received it in 1819 from Bréon, director of the Royal gardens in the Isle of Bourbon. The following account of its origin is given by Bréon, and is also mentioned by Rivers:

"At the Isle of Bourbon, the inhabitants generally inclose their land with hedges made of two rows of roses; one row of the common China Rose, the other of the Red Four Seasons. M. Perichon, a planter in the island, found in one of these hedges a young plant, differing very much from the others in its shoots and foliage. This he transplanted into his garden. It flowered the following year, and proved to be of a new race, and very different from the above two roses, which at that time were the only varieties known in the island."

Its resemblance to the Bengal Rose was, however, so strong, that it was soon considered a variety of that species. Its characteristics are, however, so entirely different from the Bengal, that we give it a separate place in our garden classification. To the French we owe nearly all the varieties of this class which have been produced from the original semi-double rose, or Bourbon Jacques, as it was called. Of these varieties, the following are distinct, and possess many charming qualities that cannot fail to gratify the amateur.

Acidalie.—One of the best light roses, being sometimes light blush, and at others white. Its autumnal bloom is its best.

Appoline.—A vigorous grower; its color is rose and pink.

Comte Bobrinsky.—A moderate grower, with a large and full crimson scarlet flower.

Duchesse de Thuringe.—Of moderate growth; its color is white, inclining to lilac.

Enfant d'Ajaccio.—A robust growing rose. As a pillar rose, or even a climber, it is perhaps the best of this group. Its flower is double, cupped, fragrant, and of a bright scarlet crimson.

Gloire de Rosaméne.—A rose of very luxuriant growth, and large foliage. It will make longer shoots in the same period than any other rose in this group, and will form a good pillar rose or climber. It is an abundant bloomer, and its flowers are cupped, large, semi-double, and of a brilliant deep scarlet.

Hermosa.—An old variety, but still one of the very best of this group. Its form is cupped, very double and perfect, and no rose blooms more abundantly, either forced or in the open ground. Its color is delicate rose. The plant is of medium growth, and well adapted for grouping or for planting in beds with Mrs. Bosanquet and Agrippina.

Imperatrice Josephine.—A very beautiful variety, blooming in immense clusters of a delicate pink. Its form is cupped, and the very robust habit of the plant makes it a good pillar rose.

Joseph Gourdon.—A moderate grower and of a reddish flesh color. One of the best.

Madame Lacharme.—A new variety, of the same habit as the preceding. Its flowers are of a rich blush, inclining to white. It blooms in clusters of beautifully formed and double flowers.

Pierre de St. Cyr.—One of the best of its color, which is rosy pink.

Queen of the Bourbons.—A very beautiful and delicate rose-colored variety, slightly tinged with buff. It is cupped, very fragrant, large, and double, and its petals are arranged with a beautiful regularity.

Sir Joseph Paxton.—A strong grower, and one of the hardiest. Its color is bright rose, tinged with crimson.

Souvenir de la Malmaison.—Altogether the most perfect and superb rose of this or any other class. It was originated by Béluze, a Frenchman. Its flowers are cupped, and of very perfect form, very double, with thick, velvety petals; they are of the largest size, often four to five inches in diameter, and their color delicate blush, with a rich tint of cream. Its large and very luxuriant foliage, compact habit, and flowers of exceeding beauty, render this one of the very finest roses known.

CHINA ROSES.

Agrippina.—Though an old rose, this is still one of the best and most popular of its class. As a forcing rose, and for an abundance of bloom, it is largely cultivated by bouquet venders. It is cupped, beautifully formed, and of a rich, brilliant crimson, with a delicate white stripe in the centre of each petal. It is one of the most hardy and desirable of the old China Roses.

Archduke Charles.—A fine cupped and hardy rose (in this class we always use *hardy* comparatively). Its color is rose, changing to crimson during expansion, and having frequently a beautiful carnation-like appearance.

Cels multiflora.—An abundant bloomer; its color is white, shaded with pink.

Daily Blush.—One of the oldest China Roses, but one of the very best. There can be nothing more perfect than its half-expanded bud, of a light crimson, inclining to blush. It commences blooming among the earliest, and, if the old seed-vessels are picked off, will continue to bloom abundantly through the summer and autumn, even after severe frosts. It is one of the hardiest of the class, and if left in this latitude unprotected during the winter, will lose no more wood than it will be necessary to cut out in the spring. It grows freely, and making a stiff, upright bush, would be well adapted for a hedge—the winter performing the office of the shears. We recollect seeing at Genoa, in Italy, a beautiful hedge of this rose, which, even at that time, in midwinter, had not lost all its foliage. We can imagine few things more beautiful than a well-cultivated hedge of this rose, with its smooth, glossy foliage, well sprinkled with the beautiful ruby-tinted buds.

Daily White.—Very similar to the preceding, in everything but the color of its flowers, which are pure white. Like the other, its fully expanded flowers are inferior to many other varieties, but its half-blown buds are very perfect, and make it a desirable plant for the bouquet-maker.

Eugene Beauharnais.—Large and double; its color is bright, a deep scarlet crimson.

General Lamoriciere.—Bright scarlet crimson, and a free bloomer.

Le Phœnix.—Distinct, fragrant, and of a deep rose color.

Louis Philippe.—A strong grower, large, double and globular. Its color is dark crimson, with blush centre.

Madame Bréon.—One of the very best. Its flowers are very large and double, beautifully cupped, and of a brilliant rose color. Few of the old China Roses can surpass it.

Mrs. Bosanquet.—One of the most desirable of the old China Roses, and there are few in any other class that are superior to it. Its growth is luxuriant, and its superb cupped, wax-like flowers are of a delicate flesh-color, and are produced in the greatest abundance.

Queen of Lombardy.—Of good size, and its color is red, passing into purple.

Sanguinea.—Rich crimson flowers, glowing like rubies. It is a free bloomer, of dwarf habit, and makes the best bedding rose known.

NOISETTE ROSES.

Aimée Vibert.—One of the most beautiful of the Noisette or cluster-flowering roses. It blooms freely through the season, is tolerably hardy, and produces an abundance of small, snow-white flowers, in fine clusters.

America.—This has large and full flowers. Its color is creamy yellow.

Chromatella.—A truly magnificent and splendid rose, raised at Angers (France), from Lamarque. It is of robust habit, and its luxuriant shoots would make it a fine pillar rose. Its leaves are large and glossy, with a beautiful, rich purple edge when young. The bud is of a rich cream color, but when the large, globular flower is fully expanded, its color is a brilliant and beautiful yellow, with petals whose thickness will endure the hottest sun without fading. When the plant is young, it is rather a shy bloomer, but when of some age, and in a good soil and location, nothing can exceed the magnificence of its superb flowers. In our grounds, it has endured our coldest winters, but it would be safer to protect it.

Caroline de Marniesse.—One of the hardiest. Its color is white, with a tinge of pink in the centre.

Celine Forestier.—A vigorous growing rose. One of the hardiest, and with a large, full flower. Its color is rich yellow.

Cornelia Koch.—This has a full and fine form. Its color is pale yellow.

Isabella Gray.—A large and full seedling of Chromatella, of a rich yellow.

Jeanne d'Arc.—A pure white rose, with a very fine form, and vigorous habit.

Lamarque.—A well-known and superb variety, whose very vigorous growth adapts it well for a pillar, or even for a climber, as in rich soils and favorable locations it will make shoots of fifteen feet in a season. When budded on a strong stock, few roses can surpass its large cupped and nearly white flowers, weighing down the stems with their weight. It is a fragrant and most desirable variety.

Madame Jouvain.—Bright rose, with a buff centre. It is very fragrant, and has a vigorous growth, adapting it for pillars.

Ophire.—A medium-sized rose, of a very singular color, entirely different from any other rose known, being a bright salmon, almost saffron. It blooms in clusters, and its luxuriant habit would make it a good pillar rose.

Solfaterre.—Another superb rose, of very much the same character. Its flowers are large and globular, inclining to flat, and their color bright lemon. When half opened, the buds are superb. Like Chromatella, (and Lamarque, the parent of both), its growth is very luxuriant. Rivers mentions a plant which threw out a shoot from a single bud eighteen feet in one season, and the next season was covered with flower-buds.

Triomphe de Rennes.—A fine rose, of large, full form, and canary color.

TEA ROSES.

Adam.—One of the finest tea-scented roses. Its flowers are cupped, very double and large, and of perfect form. It is very fragrant, and its color is a rich, glossy rose.

Abricoté.—Large and double; its color a pale fawn, with apricot centre.

Auguste Vacher.—Yellow, shaded with copper. Its form is large and full.

Barbot.—A very large, cupped rose, tea-scented, and of a beautiful fawn color.

Bougere.—A very large, superb rose, one of the very best of the tea-scented varieties. Its form is cupped, and its color a rich, glossy, bronzed rose.

Caroline.—A fine variety, with very double and perfect flowers, of a bright rose color.

Comte de Paris.—This is a superb cupped and tea-scented rose, whose magnificent size and hardy, robust nature fully compensate for its deficiency of petals, when fully expanded. Its foliage is large, its growth is very luxuriant, and its flowers of a pale rose color.

Clara Sylvain.—One of the best white roses. It grows very freely, and gives its globular, pure white, and fragrant flowers in the greatest abundance.

Devoniensis.—A very beautiful rose, of immense size. Like Chromatella, it is sometimes a shy bloomer when young, but is well adapted for forcing. Its form is cupped, and its color a fine creamy white, tinted with rose.

Duchesse d'Orleans.—Well cupped, and of a blush color.

Delphine Gaudot.—Of medium size, double and white.

Dremont.—This has a delicately tinged buff color.

David Pradel.—This variety is unique. Its color is rose, tinted with lavender, and its flowers are often of very large size.

Duc de Magenta.—Has a large and fine form. Its color is rosy salmon, shading to pink.

Eliza Sauvage.—One of the finest of the tea-scented roses. Its habit is good, its bloom is free and abundant, and its very large and double globular flowers are of a fine, pale yellow, with orange centre.

Enfant de Lyon.—Large and full, with yellow color.

Eugene Desgaches.—One of the finest Tea Roses. It is very large and full, and its bud is unsurpassed. Its color is a clear, bright rose.

Eugenie Jovin.—One of the best roses. Its flowers are large, abundant, and of a flesh-colored white, slightly tinted with fawn.

Gigantesque.—A very large and full rose, flesh-colored, and darker in the centre.

Grandiflora.—One of the most luxuriant and robust roses, and a distinct, excellent variety. Its flowers are crimson, globular, and of the largest size.

General Tartas.—This is of a dark rose color, and has a large and full form.

Gloire de Dijon.—One of the finest and hardiest of the whole group. It is a strong grower, and makes a good climber. Its foliage is luxuriant, and its flowers are large and double. Their color is pale salmon, buff, and yellow. This variety will always give satisfaction.

Homer.—A peculiar and beautiful rose when in bud. Its color is rose, tipped with red, and with a salmon centre.

Isabella Sprunt.—A new, yellow rose, of great merit. Its remarkably free blooming qualities make it a valuable acquisition for forcing and for cut flowers.

Jaune d'Or.—A golden yellow rose, of good form.

Julie Mansais.—A large and superb tea-scented rose, globular, and very fragrant. Its color is white, with lemon centre.

Lyonnais.—A large rose, and one of the hardiest of its class. It blooms freely, with a pale flesh color. Its half-opened buds are beautiful.

Louis de Savoy.—Fine yellow, with large and full form.

Madame de Vatry.—A very fine variety, with large and full form. Its color is deep rose.

Madame Bravy.—Finely formed, and of a creamy white color.

Madame Falcot.—Buff yellow, something deeper than Safrano, and more double in form. One of the best.

Madame Halphin.—Large and full, and its color is salmon pink, with a lemon centre.

Fig. 3.—MARECHAL NIEL.

Madame de Tartas.—Large, and free blooming, of a bright rose color.

Madame Villermoz.—A very fine, large variety. Its color is creamy white, tinted with fawn, with a salmon centre.

Maréchal Niel.—A vigorous growing rose, more free blooming than Chromatella. Its color is yellow, deepening at the centre to a rich, golden yellow. It is, perhaps, the largest and most beautiful yellow rose known, and very fragrant.

Marquise de Foucault.—Has a large white flower, with yellow centre. Its habit is vigorous.

Niphetos.—Has long and pointed buds, of a pale straw color. It blooms best in dry weather.

Pactole.—One of the very best of its class. Its form is cupped, and its color pale sulphur, with a deep yellow centre. It blooms very abundantly, and is robust and hard. It is one of the best roses for forcing, and for bouquets.

President.—A fine, large, and well-formed rose. Its color is rose, shaded with salmon.

Polonie Bordin.—Creamy salmon, with yellow centre, and full form.

Rubens.—Color rose and white, with yellow centre. Form large and double.

Safrano.—This is scarcely excelled by any rose. Its half-opened bud is very beautiful, and of a rich, deep fawn color. When open, its form is cupped, and its color a much lighter fawn. These fawn-colored roses have peculiar charms for us; and of them all, there are none more beautiful or richer than Safrano.

Silene.—A very beautiful tea-scented rose, cupped, very double, and fragrant. Its color is rose, shaded with crimson, and the plant is hardy and of luxuriant growth.

Sombreuil.—A strong grower, with flowers of a pale straw color.

Souvenir d'un Ami.—The queen of the tea-scented roses, and will rank the very first among them. Its habit is good, it blooms freely, and its large and beautifully imbricated flowers, when open, much resemble in form those of Souvenir de Malmaison. Its color is a delicate salmon, shaded with rose, and its general character highly recommends it as first-rate in every respect. Hibberd claims to have produced flowers from this variety eleven to twelve inches in circumference when fully expanded.

Souvenir de Leveson Gower.—Of a salmon color.

Triomphe de Guillot fils.—A white rose, clouded with flesh color, and shaded with yellowish salmon.

Vicomtesse de Cazes.—A fine yellow, and free blooming rose.

White Tea.—A well-cupped, fragrant, pure white rose.

In the preceding list, we have given some of the best varieties of the Tea Rose, and trust the amateur will find no difficulty in making a selection. Many are pillar roses; and these, so trained, would be beautiful objects on a lawn, either singly, or in groups of three to a dozen. Where the height of the pillars can be gently graduated to the highest in the centre, the effect will be very fine. Many of the luxuriant growing varieties can be trained upon a common pale fence, and will cover it with flowers and foliage the whole season. Straw can be easily thatched over to protect them from the severity of winter, or bass mats would be still better. There is another very beautiful mode of cultivating the most delicate of these tea-scented roses, which we have never seen adopted, but which we are confident would produce a very fine effect. A large three or four gallon pot should be procured, and painted green on the outside; a locust post should then be obtained. some three or four inches in diameter, and five to twelve feet in height, according to the usual length of the shoots of the variety of rose to be planted. Upon the top of this post can be placed a circular or square piece of board, the diameter of the bottom of the pot. The post should then be planted firmly in the ground and painted green. Fill the pot with rich soil, as directed in a preceding chapter; plant in it one or two roses of pillar varieties, and place it on the top of the post. The surface of the soil should then be covered with moss, and if the sides can also be covered, the good effect will be enhanced. The plants, if strong, will soon throw out long, graceful shoots, which, drooping to the ground, will hide the pot and post, and present the appearance of an everblooming weeping tree of great beauty. If a pyramid is desired, wires can be carried from the top of the post to the ground, some two or three feet from its base, and the shoots trained down these. We can imagine few things more beautiful than Chromatella and Solfaterre, growing and blooming in this way.

MACARTNEY ROSES.

The Macartney rose was brought from China to England by Lord Macartney, in 1793. Its habit is luxuriant, and its foliage is more beautiful than that of any other rose, its leaves being thick, and of a rich, glossy green. It commences blooming about midsummer, and its flowers, with a fragrance like the perfume of an apricot, succeed each other without interruption till the first frosts, while the leaves remain till the very latest. Although as hardy as the hardiest of the China Roses, it would be better in this latitude to give it the same protection as recommended for the China. It is one of the most desirable roses for beds or borders. When covering the whole ground, and kept well pegged down, its rich, glossy foliage, gemmed with fragrant flowers, produces a beautiful effect. The varieties of this rose are very few, but the best two are the following:

Alba odorata.—A vigorous growing rose, with very rich and beautiful foliage. Its fragrant flowers are cream-colored, and, when in bud, are very beautiful. It has stood the last three winters uninjured in our grounds, without protection, and is a very beautiful and desirable variety. It is classed by Rivers as a Microphylla, but it so little resembles that rose, and is so decidedly Macartney in its character, that we place it with the latter.

Maria Leonida.—A very beautiful, but not entirely double variety, as its stamens can sometimes be seen, which, however, give a graceful appearance. Its flowers are finely cupped, and pure white, with a tinge of blush at the base of the petals.

MICROPHYLLA ROSES.

This species, originally from the Himalayan Mountains, was first brought to Europe in 1823. Its foliage is small and singular, and its growth is very robust. Its flowers bloom from midsummer till frost, and have a striking appearance; they are very double, with a calyx of which the small, bristling sepals give the opening bud the appearance of a small chestnut. The plant is hardy, and has endured the winter in our grounds for the past twenty years without protection, losing only a portion of the tops of its shoots. Of the several varieties, one of the best is

Rubra, which has very double and cupped flowers, of a blush and often rose color, with a deep red centre.

MUSK ROSES.

The Musk Rose grows naturally in Persia and other Eastern countries, where it attains the height of a small tree, and is doubtless the rose which has been celebrated by Eastern poets. It is also found in India, where it is probably the species used for making attar. In this latitude it is quite hardy, and we have a plant of the old White Musk in our grounds, that has braved the severity of more than twenty winters. It has made in one season shoots more than six feet long, and in our Southern States, more than double the growth would probably be obtained. The blossoms appear in clusters, and commencing later than any other rose, continue abundant throughout the season. The Old White Cluster has been widely distributed throughout the country, and is deservedly a favorite. The best two varieties, however, are the following:

Eponine.—A cupped and very double variety, with the peculiar musk fragrance. It is pure white, and a very pretty rose.

Princess of Nassau.—A luxuriant growing and very fragrant variety, and would make a good pillar rose. It blooms in large clusters of cupped flowers, changing from yellow to cream color as they open.

ROSES THAT BLOOM ONLY ONCE IN THE SEASON.

GARDEN ROSES.

For want of a better, we use this term to designate all those roses that bloom only once in the season, and that strongly resemble each other in habit and flower. It includes those classes called, by rose-growers, French, Provence, Hybrid Provence, Hybrid China, Hybrid Bourbon, White and Damask Roses.

On a preceding page, we have given our opinion respecting classification, but we wish it to be fully understood, that we do not deny the existence of clearly distinctive characters in the true French, Provence, Damask, etc., but simply assert that the lines of difference between these so run into each other, and are so blended together,

Fig. 4.—GARDEN ROSE.

that it is almost impossible to know where to place a new rose, which may partake of the qualities of all. We have mentioned Rivers as the most skillful and correct of rose-growers; and yet, in classing Lady Fitzgerald and Madame Hardy among the Damasks, he says that neither of them are pure Damask; and the Duke of Cambridge, which at first he thought a Hybrid China, he now places as a Damask; other similar instances are frequent. Many roses, moreover, are classed as hybrids which are not truly such. We are quite inclined to think that a large number of the varieties supposed to have been produced by hybridizing are nothing more than the natural produce, and that the pollen, in many cases, has not impregnated the pistil to which it was applied. With this uncertainty, therefore, as evinced by Rivers in his work, and with doubts of the hybridity of supposed hybrids, we deem it better to class them all together; and, for the benefit of those who may prefer the old classification, to attach to each name the class by which it has been hitherto known.

We write principally for the amateur, and we think he will find it less embarrassing to make a selection from this classification than from the old one.

A great number of Garden Roses exist, but we describe here only a few distinct varieties, with colors which are seldom found among the Remontants.

All the others have either their equals or their superiors among the Remontants, and being certain to bloom only once in the season, are scarcely worthy of cultivation, compared with the Remontants.

Chénédole, H. C.—One of the most splendid varieties, and is truly beautiful. Its foliage and habit are very good, and its very luxuriant growth makes it a good pillar rose. Its flower is cupped, large, double, and fragrant, and its color is a rich, glowing crimson, of almost dazzling brilliancy. It is altogether the most desirable rose of this class.

Charles Lawson, H. B.—This has handsome foliage,

and vigorous habit of growth, with large, symmetrical, and bright rose-colored flowers.

Coupe d'Hébé, H. B.—A gem of the family. It is large, double, symmetrical, and finely cupped. Its color a delicate, wax-like, rosy pink. Its growth is luxuriant, and adapted for pillars.

Emerance, H. P.—A beautiful cupped rose, of a color unusual in this class, being of a pale lemon or straw color. Its form is very regular, and the habit of the plant good.

George the Fourth, H. C.—An old rose, produced by T. Rivers, but is still one of the most desirable of this class. Its flowers are of a dark crimson, and its young shoots have a purple tinge. Its very luxuriant habit makes it suitable for a pillar.

Julie d'Etranges, F.—This has a large cupped flower, of a delicate rose color.

Madame Hardy, F.—A vigorous habit, and finely shaped flower. Its color is pure white, sometimes with a green centre.

Madame Plantier, H. C.—A cupped and double pure white rose. It is a luxuriant grower, a most abundant bloomer, and one of the very best of the white summer roses. Its foliage is so marked in its richness and beauty that any one can readily distinguish it by that alone. Were it Remontant, it would possess all the requisites of a perfect white rose.

Obscurité, F.—One of the darkest roses known.

Œillet Parfait, F.—A beautiful striped rose, resembling a carnation. Its form is compact, and its color a very light blush, nearly white, beautifully and distinctly striped with rose and bright crimson.

Tricolor de Flandre, F.—A very double, distinct, and compact flower. Its color is lilac, striped with red and crimson.

MOSS ROSES.

The Moss Rose was introduced into England from Holland in the sixteenth century, and is first mentioned by Miller, in 1727, by whom it was supposed to be a sport of the Provence Rose, which opinion has been confirmed by modern botanists. Its peculiarities are the delicate prickles which crowd its stem, and the beautiful mossy covering of its calyx. This mossy appearance has been deemed by some a mere *lusus naturæ*, and by others the work of an insect similar to that which produces the Bédéguar, or Rose-gall. The former opinion, however, prevails; and this freak of nature cultivators have succeeded in fixing and perpetuating in a great number of varieties. The first Moss Rose known in France was said to have been introduced there by Madame de Genlis, who brought it with her on her return from England. In 1810, scarcely more than one variety was known, and now there exist more than a hundred. Of these, the best and most distinct are the following:

A Feuilles Pourpres.—A distinct rose. The flower is bright red, and the young leaves are red.

Baronne de Wassenaer.—This has a good form, bright red color, and flowers in clusters.

Captain Ingram.—Flowers of a dark, velvety purple.

Comtesse de Murinais.—A vigorous habit. Its color is pale flesh, changing to pure white, and it is one of the best of the white Mosses.

Common.—This is the old Rose-colored Moss, which has been generally cultivated in gardens. It grows well, blooms freely, is well covered with moss, and is one of the best of the old varieties.

Cristata.—A very singular and beautiful variety, said to have been discovered in the crevice of a wall at Friburg, in Switzerland. Rivers classes it with the Provence

Roses, and when open, it is merely a variety of that rose; but when in bud, it is more properly a Moss, although its calyx is not covered with a fine moss, but has more of a crested appearance. In a rich soil this fringe-like crest most beautifully clasps and surmounts the bud, and gives the rich clusters a truly elegant appearance. Its form is globular, and its color rose. It is one of the few that do not grow well on their own roots, but require to be budded on some strong-growing stock.

Diane de Castre.—Of a light rose color.

Duchesse d'Istrie.—Of medium size, and with a bright rose color.

Eugene de Savoie.—This was described among the Remontant Mosses.

Gloire des Mousseuses.—A large and handsome flower, with a clear, pale rose color.

Hooker's Blush.—A cupped rose, blooming in large clusters of a blush color.

Hortense Vernet.—Flowers of a dark rose color.

Jenny Lind.—A small or medium-sized rose-colored flower.

Laneii.—A vigorous grower, and has large and thrifty foliage. The buds are large and well mossed, and it is beautiful both in bud and expanded. Its color is bright rose.

Luxembourg.—Like the last, of vigorous growth. Its flowers are a purplish crimson.

Madame de Rochelambert.—This has large and full flowers, of an amaranth color.

Madame Edouard Ory.—This was described among the Remontant Mosses.

Nuits de Young.—Plant of a dwarf habit. Its flowers are small, with a deep, velvety purple color.

Princesse Adelaide.—A remarkably vigorous-growing

variety, with large and handsome foliage, and would make a good pillar rose. Its regularly formed flowers, of a bright pink or rose, are produced in clusters, and open well. It does not bear close pruning. This is one of the most desirable of its class, and owes its origin to Laffay.

Princess Royal.—A very robust rose, almost equal to the preceding in vigor. Its young leaves and branches have a red tinge, and its cupped flowers are of a deep crimson purple, marbled and spotted with red. Although not quite double when fully open, they are very beautiful when in bud. A moss rose, however double, is peculiar only in bud, for, when fully expanded, the mossy calyx must inevitably be hidden.

Perpetual White.—This was described among the Remontant Mosses, as also were

Raphael, and
Salet.

William Lobb.—A good growing plant, with double flowers. Its color is carmine, shaded with violet.

Like all other roses, and even in a greater degree, the Moss Rose requires a light and very rich soil, with a dry bottom. Many of them make very beautiful beds and patches, when planted in rich soil, and kept well pegged down. A good supply of stable manure should be given them in the autumn, to be washed down about their roots by the winter rains. They do not generally require or bear so much pruning as other roses, but their bloom may sometimes be prolonged by shortening part of the shoots close, and only the tips of the remainder. When properly cultivated, few objects can be more beautiful than these roses, either singly or in masses. Without making so brilliant a show as some other classes, the moss which envelops them imparts a touch of graceful beauty belonging to no other flower.

SCOTCH ROSES.

These roses are all derived from a dwarf rose found growing wild in Scotland and in the north of England. They are distinguished by their small leaves, abundant bloom, and delicate habit. Being perfectly hardy, they are desirable for beds or borders, in which, with proper arrangement of colors, they show beautifully, sometimes two weeks before other roses open, producing flowers all along the stem. Rose growers describe, in their catalogues, two or three hundred varieties, but of them all, scarcely forty or fifty are distinct; of these the best three are the following:

Countess of Glasgow.—A very pretty and brilliant dark rose, blooming abundantly.

Queen of May.—A fine and distinct variety, of a bright pink color.

William the Fourth.—An excellent variety, of luxuriant growth. Its flowers are pure white, and among the largest of the class.

BRIER ROSES.

These roses are distinguished by their small, rough foliage and brier habit. They include the Sweet-Brier, the Hybrid Sweet-Brier, and the Austrian Brier. The Sweet-Brier is found in various parts of this country and in Europe, and is distinguished by the peculiar delightful fragrance of its leaves. Its simple little flower, found among the hedges, has been long a favorite, and, under the name of Eglantine, has been often the theme of poets.

The Hybrid Sweet-Brier is allied to the preceding, but has larger foliage, and is of more robust growth. Many roses have been placed in this class and among the Sweet-Briers that have none of the peculiar scent of the Sweet-Briers; and hence, again, the necessity of classing together these and the Austrian Briers, respecting which there is much confusion. The true Austrian Rose is a native of the South of Europe, and is a clearly distinct rose; but some have been called Austrian which have scarcely any of the characters of the original rose. All three, however, are Briers, that is, they produce their flowers on short joints all along the stem, and have the peculiar rough, briery leaves. We therefore place them all together, attaching as before the name of the old class. The best are the following:

Celestial, S. B.—A small cupped rose, very double and fragrant, of a pale flesh-color and very pretty.

Copper Austrian, A. B.—A very singular looking rose, blooming well in this climate. The inside of the flower is of a coppery-red, and the outside inclining to pale yellow or sulphur. It is desirable for its peculiar color.

Double Margined Hip, H. S. B.—Of luxuriant growth, almost adapted for a pillar. Its form is cupped, and its color creamy-white, shaded with pink.

Double Yellow Provence is the best of the two varieties which compose the species called Sulphurea. We have never seen its flowers, and English writers all speak of the great difficulty of making it bloom. Rivers recommends to bud it on strong stocks, and says that it blooms most profusely in the warm, dry climate of Florence and Genoa. The plant grows with luxuriance and produces plenty of flower-buds, which, with proper culture, would probably open in our warm climate, which is very similar to that of Florence and Genoa. Its small foliage and slender, thorny wood, place it fairly among the Briers. Its flower is so fine that it is well worth the trouble of repeated experiment to obtain a good bloom. It has long been admired and exercised the skill of rose growers, as is proved by the following passages from some old works, which give instructions for proper culture:

"Whereas all other roses are best natural, this is best inoculated upon another stock. Others thrive and bear best in the sun; this, in the shade: therefore the best way that I know to cause this rose to bring forth fair and kindly flowers, is performed after this manner. First in the stock of a Francfort Rose, near the ground, put in the bud of the single yellow rose, which will quickly shoot to a good length; then, half a yard higher than the place where the same was budded, put into it a bud of the double yellow rose, which growing, the suckers must be kept from the root, and all the buds rubbed off, except those of the kind desired, which, being grown big enough to bear (which will be in two years), it must in winter be pruned very near, cutting off all the small shoots, and only leaving the biggest, cutting off the tops of them also, as far as they are small. Then in the spring, when the buds for leaves come forth, rub off the smallest of them, leaving only some few of the biggest, which, by reason of the strength of the stock, affordeth more nourishment than any other, and the agreeable nature of the single yellow rose, from whence it is immediately nourished, the shoots will be strong and able to bear out the flowers, if they be not too many, which may be prevented by nipping off the smallest buds for flowers. The tree should stand something shadowed, and not too much in the heat of the sun, and in a standard by itself, rather than under a wall." That which follows is from a book called *Systema Horticulturæ*, dated 1688:—"There is no flower-bearing tree that yields blossom so beautiful as the rose, whereof the yellow Provence Rose is the most beautiful where it brings forth fair and kindly flowers, which hath been obtained by budding a single yellow rose on the stock of a flourishing Francfort Rose near the ground: when that single yellow is well grown, in that branch inoculate your double yellow rose; then cut off all suckers and shoots from the first and second, leaving only your last, which must be pruned very near, leaving but few buds, which will have the more nourishment, and yield the fairer and more entire blossoms. This tree, or a layer from a rose of the same kind, delights most, and blows fairest, in a cold, moist, and shady place, and not against a hot wall."

Harrisonii.—A fine yellow Brier of American origin, and is perhaps the best hardy yellow rose for general cultivation.

Persian Yellow, A. B.—This is the deepest yellow rose known, and is a highly improved edition of the Harrison. Its flowers are more double, and of a deeper yellow than that rose. It grows freely, blooms abundantly, and its small double flowers possess a richness of color unequaled by any other rose. No garden should be without it. It should be added, however, that it is exceedingly difficult to strike from cuttings, and is one of those few varieties for which budding upon another stock is preferable.

Rose Angle, S. B. — An excellent variety, with very fragrant foliage, and large double flowers of a bright rose color. It is one of the best of the true Eglantines.

Like the Moss Roses, the Briers will not bear much pruning, and require merely the tips of the shoots to be cut off.

AYRSHIRE ROSES.

This class is very valuable for covering unsightly places, old buildings, and decayed trees. They bloom some two weeks earlier than other roses, and will grow in soil where others would scarcely vegetate. Hence they are valuable for covering naked sand-banks, or bare spots of earth, and their roots would be of material assistance in keeping up the soil of loose banks. Rivers gives an extract from the Dundee Courier, showing the effect produced by some of these roses.

"Some years ago, a sand pit at Ellangowan was filled up with rubbish found in digging a well. Over this a piece of rock was formed for the growth of plants which prefer such situations, and among them were planted some half dozen plants of the Double Ayrshire Rose, raised in this neighborhood about ten years ago. These roses now most completely cover the whole ground, a space of thirty feet by twenty. At present they are in full bloom, showing probably not less than ten thousand roses in this small space."

The Ayrshire Roses are also valuable for weeping trees; when budded on a stock some ten or twelve feet high, the branches quickly reach the ground, and protecting the stem from the sun by their close foliage, present a weeping tree of great beauty, loaded with flowers.

Dundee Rambler.—One of the best and most double of the Ayrshire Roses. Its color is white, often edged with pink, and blooming in large clusters. It is a very desirable variety.

Double Blush Ayrshire.—A most vigorous climber, with a pretty flower, and will grow in the poorest soil.

BANKSIAN ROSES.

Roses of this class have a very small flower closely resembling that of the double *Spiræa prunifolia*, and blooming in clusters of about the same size. In this climate they require the protection of a green-house, and are very striking for the great profusion of their corymbs of pure white or deep yellow flowers. We recollect seeing, at the Botanic Garden at Naples, a very large plant of the Banksian Rose, the main stem being six inches in diameter, and branching off into a dozen others, fifty feet or more long. In the Southern States they would grow well in the open air, and being most vigorous climbers, would soon cover a house or trellis, and, with their small but most abundant flowers interspersed among the smooth glossy-green foliage, would form an object of great beauty.

Double White.—Introduced into England from China in 1807, and named in honor of Lady Banks. It is a beautiful little rose about half an inch in diameter, blooming abundantly in small and pure white clusters with a slight perfume like that of the violet.

Double Yellow.—Introduced in 1827. It has bright buff-yellow flowers; these are produced in great abundance, and give a pleasant perfume before the dew is off early in the morning, or just at evening.

Fortuniana.—Introduced by Fortune in 1850. It has white fragrant flowers of much larger size than the preceding varieties. Its want of the *petite* character of the others makes it less beautiful and striking.

Jaune Serin.—A luxuriant growing variety, with yellow flowers of larger size than those of the old Yellow Banksia.

The Banksian Roses do not bear much pruning. It should be done immediately after the bloom is over, and then only the heavier branches cut out, leaving those which are full of flower-bearing twigs, which should not be shortened. If the branches are all shortened, the plants will produce an abundance of strong, new wood, but no flowers.

BOURSAULT ROSES.

This class is marked by its long, flexible, reddish shoots, which grow rapidly, and are perfectly hardy. Their smooth bark renders them desirable for stocks to bud upon, and a fine rose of this class, covering a trellis and budded with roses of various colors, would present a beautiful appearance. These, also, are impatient of much pruning.

Amadis.—One of the best, with its pendulous clusters of large purplish-crimson flowers.

Blush.—This has large, double, blush flowers.

EVERGREEN ROSES.

The original of this class is the *Rosa sempervirens*, a wild rose of Italy. They are very beautiful and desirable, and although not entirely evergreen in this climate, retain their foliage very late in the season. They are very easy of cultivation, and most luxuriant climbers over naked trees, old houses, fences, and walls, or along the surface of the ground, which they will soon cover to the exclusion of all weeds, and present a large mass of rich, glossy foliage, and abundant bloom. When thus planted, the large weeds should be pulled up until the plant fairly covers the ground, when no more attention will be needed. They are well adapted for training up columns, and we know of few things more beautiful than a temple formed of numerous columns, with Evergreen Roses growing luxuriantly upon them and festooned gracefully between. Nothing, indeed, can be more gracefully beautiful than festoons, wherever they can be made. They constitute the chief beauty of the vine-clad fields of Italy, and there would be no less beauty in occasional festooning of roses trained between pillars or the trees of a lawn. They are also very beautiful when budded on high standards, their dark-green glossy foliage weeping to the ground, and forming a fine dome or pyramid of leaf and bloom. When pruned in the winter, the branches may be thinned out, but not shortened; for if pruned close, they will make a luxuriant growth the next season, but will produce no flowers.

Félicité Perpetuelle.—A most beautiful rose, and one of the very best of the class; when properly cultivated, it produces an abundance of very double creamy-white flowers, shaped like a double ranunculus.

Melanie de Montjoie.—A variety of much beauty. Its abundant and glossy dark-green foliage contrasts beautifully with its large, pure white flowers.

Myrianthes.—One of the best of this class. Its flowers are perfectly shaped, and of a very delicate rose color.

Triomphe de Bollwiller.—A very fine hybrid between the Evergreen and Tea Roses. It is rather tender in this climate, but valuable for its tendency to bloom in the autumn. Its flowers are very large, double, fragrant, and globular, and their color is a blush or creamy white. At the South, where it would not be killed by the cold weather, this would be one of the most desirable climbing roses.

HYBRID CLIMBING ROSES.

We include here some which do not belong to any of the distinct classes.

Indica Major.—A hybrid climbing rose, of most luxuriant growth and nearly evergreen foliage. Its flowers are very large, double, and of a delicate rose color. The very rapid growth of this rose makes it excellent for covering old buildings. We recollect being shown, at the Bartram garden of Philadelphia, a fine old plant which had covered the whole side of the house, and presented a beautiful appearance. Buist states it to be this variety.

Madame d'Arblay is a truly gigantic hybrid climber, perfectly hardy, and with strong, Bourbon-like foliage. It blooms in large clusters of pure white flowers, and is a truly excellent variety.

Menoux.—This variety has crimson flowers, a color which is not common among climbing roses.

Sir John Sebright.—A hybrid Musk rose, grown by

Rivers. Its flowers are produced in large clusters, are very fragrant, and their color is a bright crimson-scarlet.

The Garland.—A most vigorous hybrid climber, blooming in immense clusters of fragrant, creamy-white flowers, changing to blush after expansion. When in full bloom, the contrast of the large white clusters with the bright green foliage is very beautiful.

MULTIFLORA ROSES.

The parent of this class is a native of China and Japan. They are unfortunately somewhat tender in this climate. We have known them to endure safely several winters when unprotected, but they are unreliable in this respect. One of the best is

Grevillei or Seven Sisters.—It has a remarkably vigorous growth, and blooms with unusual profusion. A large plant will not unfrequently show more than a thousand flowers, all blooming in clusters and of several shades of color. This variety is impatient of much pruning.

De la Grifferaie.—This bears the knife better than the preceding, and may be grown as a bush with proper pruning. It is hardier than others of the class, and bears a profusion of blush and rose-colored flowers.

Laure Davoust.—One of the most beautiful of the Multiflora Roses, and of most luxuriant growth. It has larger flowers and handsomer foliage than any of the other Multiflora Roses, and blooms in immense clusters of perfect flowers, changing from white to pink. For covering houses or trellises it is very desirable.

Russelliana.—This is very vigorous, and yet bears pruning so well that it may be grown as a bush. Its clusters are large, and the flowers change as they open from dark to light red lilac, giving it a singular appearance.

THE PRAIRIE ROSE.

The double varieties of the original Michigan Rose, or *Rosa rubifolia*, have nearly all been produced by Samuel Feast, of Baltimore, while a few new varieties owe their origin to Joshua Pierce, of Washington. They are remarkable for their perfectly hardy nature, braving equally well the frosts of Canada or the heat of Louisiana. The leaves are large, rather rough, and of a rich dark-green. They grow with unexampled rapidity, exceeding in this respect any of the climbing roses, and would cover old buildings or naked ground in a very short space of time. They bloom after the other summer roses are mostly gone, and produce their flowers abundantly in large clusters of different shades, from the shaded white of Baltimore Belle to the rich deep rose of

Queen of the Prairies.—This is the best, and of the most luxuriant growth. Its large flowers are of a peculiar cupped form, almost globular, when in bud, and altogether of very perfect shape. They are of a deep rose color, with a white stripe in the centre of each petal. This rose is truly superb, and, for our cold winters and hot sun, an unequaled climber. It would be a fine rose to cover a trellis or building, and then bud into its branches a dozen different Remontant or Bourbon Roses of various colors. The *tout ensemble* would be superb.

Baltimore Belle.—This variety is thought by some to have a strain of Noisette sap in it from the delicacy and beauty of its flower and its tendency to bloom in the autumn. It produces abundant clusters of white flowers shaded with a slight cloud of pink. It is one of the finest climbing roses known.

Gem of the Prairie. (Burgess'.)—A hybrid between the Queen of the Prairies and the Remontant, Madame Laffay. It is said to combine the vigorous growth of the one with the rich color and delicate fragrance of the other. We have not grown this variety, but take the description from the Horticultural Annual for 1868.

Jane.—Very double, of a deep rosy lilac.

Mrs. Hovey.—This has large white flowers, and all the vigor of its class.

Pride of Washington.—A rosy lilac, and double.

There are several other varieties in this class, but the preceding are the best.

CHAPTER III.

GENERAL CULTURE OF THE ROSE.

As before stated, the Rose was the theme of the earliest poets of antiquity; and it was doubtless one of the first plants selected to adorn the gardens which were laid out around the new habitations constructed upon the exchange of the wandering for a civilized mode of life.

The most ancient authors upon husbandry, whose works are extant, have all treated of the culture of Roses: Theophrastus among the Greeks; and among the Romans, Varro, Columella, Palladius, and Pliny. To Pliny are we specially indebted for information on this subject, as the entire fourth chapter of the twentieth book of his Natural History is devoted to Roses; and they are also occasionally mentioned in other parts of the work. But after all the information thus obtained, much yet remains to be desired; and although we find in other ancient authors some curious facts bearing upon other points in the history of the Rose, they are mostly so general in their character as to give us very little insight into the actual culture of the Rose at those periods.

The profuseness with which they were used among the Greeks, the Romans, the Egyptians, and other ancient nations in their religious solemnities, their public ceremonies, and even in the ordinary customs of private life, would lead us to suppose, and with some degree of correctness, that roses were very abundantly cultivated by them all; and we are inclined to think that their cultivation was then far more general than at the present time, although the art of producing them was in its infancy. However surprising in other respects may have been the progress of the culture of roses within forty years, particularly in France, Holland, and Belgium, there can be little doubt that, although the Romans were acquainted with a much smaller number of varieties than the moderns, yet flowers of those varieties were far more abundant than the aggregate quantity of flowers of all the varieties of roses cultivated at the present day. It cannot be positively asserted that the Remontant Roses of the present time were unknown at Rome, since the gardeners of that city practiced sowing the seeds of the Rose, by which mode many of the most remarkable varieties of that class have been obtained by modern cultivators. The Romans, however, preferred to propagate by cuttings, which produced flowering plants much sooner than those from the seed.

But, though the Romans may have had roses of the same species with some of those which we now cultivate, it is scarcely probable that these species could have continued until this period, and escaped the devastation attendant on the revolutions of empire, or the more desolating invasions of the Huns and Goths. Thus it is, that those roses of Pæstum, to which allusion is so frequently made by ancient writers, and which, according to Virgil and Pliny, bloomed semi-annually, and were common in the gardens of that city, are not now to be found. Jussieu and Loudresse, two French gentlemen, successively visited Italy with the express object of finding this twice-bearing Rose in Pæstum or its environs, yet, notwithstanding their carefully prosecuted researches, they could find no traces of it whatever.

Although the number of varieties known to the Romans was very limited, they had discovered a method of making the blooming season continue many months. According to Pliny, the roses of Carthage, in Spain, came forward early and bloomed in winter; those of Campania bloomed next in order; then those of Malta; and lastly those of Pæstum, which flowered in the spring and autumn. It was probably the blooming of this last species which the gardeners of Rome discovered (in Seneca's time) the secret of retarding by a certain process, or of hastening by means of their warm green-houses.

In the first part of this work, we have cited many passages from ancient authors, which show to what an enormous extent the use of roses was carried by the Romans on certain occasions. It is difficult to credit, at this day, the relation of Nero's extravagance (which is, however, attested by Suetonius), when it is told that in one fête alone he expended in roses *only*, more than four millions of sesterces, or one hundred thousand dollars. It would be no easy matter, even at the present period of abundant cultivation of Roses, to obtain from all the nurseries of England, France, and America together, roses sufficient to amount to so large a sum.

The Romans derived the use of this flower from the Greeks. In Greece, and throughout the East, roses were cultivated, not only for the various purposes we have mentioned, but also for the extraction of their perfumes. Among the many plans which they adopted for preserving the flower was that of cutting off the top of a reed, splitting it down a short distance, and enclosing in it a number of rose-buds, which, being bound around with papyrus, prevented their fragrance from escaping. The

Greeks also deemed it a great addition to the fragrance of the Rose to plant garlic near its roots. The island of Rhodes, which has successively borne many names, was particularly indebted to the culture of roses for that which it bears at this day. It was the Isle of Roses, the Greek for Rose being Ροδον,—Rodon.

Medals of Rhodes, whose reverse impressions present a rose in bloom on one side, and the sunflower on the other, are to be found even now in cabinets of curiosities.

Extravagance in roses, among the Romans, kept pace with the increase of their power, until they at length desired them at all seasons. At first they procured their winter's supply from Egypt, but subsequently attained themselves such skill in their culture as to produce them in abundance, even at the coldest season of the year; and, according to Seneca, by means of green-houses, heated by pipes filled with hot water. During the reign of Domitian, the forcing of roses was carried to such perfection, and flowers produced in winter in so great abundance, that those brought from Egypt, as before mentioned, excited only the contempt of the citizens of the world's metropolis.

This fact, as also handed down to us by the epigram of Martial, is of great assistance in estimating the importance of rose-culture at that period, and in showing how the art of cultivating this plant had spread, and how it was already far advanced among the ancient Romans and their contemporaries.

If the Egyptians cultivated roses for transportation to Rome during the winter, they must have had very extensive plantations for the purpose. The exportation could not have been of loose flowers, for they would have been withered long before the termination of the voyage; neither could it have been of rooted plants in a dormant state, as nurserymen now send them to every part of the world, because the Romans had at that time no means of causing them to vegetate and bloom in the winter. On the contrary, the cultivators at Alexandria and Memphis must, of necessity, have sent them away in the vases and boxes in which they had planted them with that object, and when they were just beginning to break from the bud, in order that they might arrive at Rome at the moment they commenced expanding.

At that remote period, when navigation was far behind its present state of perfection, the voyage from the mouth of the Nile to the coast of Italy occupied more than twenty days. When this long voyage is considered, and also the quantity of roses required by the Romans to enwreath their crowns and garlands, to cover their tables and couches, and the pavements of their festive halls, and to surround the urns which contained the ashes of their dead, it is evident that the Egyptians, who traded in roses, in order to satisfy the prodigality of the Romans, would be compelled to keep in readiness a certain number of vessels to be laden with boxes or vases of rose-plants, so prepared as not to bloom before their delivery at Rome. The cost of roses thus delivered in Rome must have been immense, but we do not find a single passage in any of the ancient authors which can give any light on this point; they only tell us that nothing for the gratification of luxury was considered too costly by the wealthy Roman citizens. Nor do they afford more positive information as to the species of Rose cultivated on the borders of the Nile, to gratify this taste of the Romans. According to Delile, there were found in Egypt, at the time of the French expedition into that country, only the White Rose and the Centifolia, or hundred-leaved—two species not very susceptible of either a forcing or retarding culture. The only Rose known at that time, which bloomed in the winter, was the Rose of Pæstum, referred to by Virgil, as "*biferique rosaria Pæsti*," and which was probably the same as our monthly Damask Rose, and which produced in Egypt and Rome flowers at all seasons, as the Damask does now with us, under a proper mode of culture.

The extent to which the culture and commerce of roses was carried among the Romans is shown by the fact that, although they had confounded the tree and its flowers under one name—that of *Rosa*,—they nevertheless gave particular appellations to the gardens or ground planted with rose-bushes. They were termed a *Rosarium*, or a *Rosetum*. Ovid says, " *Quot amœna Rosaria flores*." The dealer in roses was also designated by the distinctive appellation of *Rosarius*.

In the latter part of the decline of the Roman Empire, when paganism still existed to a great degree, there arose a people who formed, as it were, the connecting link between the ancient and modern world—a people who acknowledged but one Supreme Ruler, and his sole vicegerent, Mahomet; a people whose origin was among the wildest tribes of Ishmael's descendants, who possessed in a great degree the luxuries of civilized life, and among whom the arts, sciences, and agriculture, were very flourishing for many ages. Among the Moors of Spain, the culture of the Rose was pursued with as much scientific and practical method as at the present day, but with somewhat less happy results. When in Paris, some years since, we became acquainted with M. Hardy, the chief director of the Luxembourg gardens, and who is well known to rose growers, by the many beautiful varieties which he has originated. His interest in this subject was very great, and in 1828, he published in the *Journal des Jardins* some interesting observations which he had extracted from a manuscript of M. de la Neuville. The latter having been employed as military superintendent in Spain during the war of 1823, translated from a Spanish version some parts of an Arabian work upon culture in general, in which that of the Rose was mentioned, with some important particulars. It stated that the Moors, who formerly conquered Spain, attached the highest value to this most beautiful of their flowers, and cultivated it with as much care as we do ourselves. "According to Abu-el-Jaïr," says the translation, "there are roses of many colors — carnation white, fallow or yellow, lapis-lazuli, or sky-blue. Some are of this last color on the outside, and yellow within. In the East they are acquainted with roses which are variegated with yellow and sky-blue, the inside of the corolla being of the one color, and the outside the other. The yellow-heart is very common in Tripoli and Syria, and the blue-heart is found on the coast of Alexandria." To us, at the present day, this relation may with reason seem incredible, since amid the numerous varieties now existing, and the skill of their cultivators, we have in no instance been able to obtain a blue Rose. Abu-el-Jaïr may have ventured to state it as a fact without proper authority, for, according to M. de la Neuville, Abu-Abdallah-ebu-el-Fazel, another nearly contemporaneous author, enumerated a variety of roses without mentioning the blue. "There are," says this last author, "four varieties of roses: the first is named the Double White; it has an exquisite odor, and its cup unites more than a hundred petals: the second is the Yellow, which is of a golden color, and bright as the jonquil; then the Purple; and lastly the flesh-colored, which is the most common of them all." Farther on the same author adds: "The number of species is supposed to be large: the Mountain or Wild; the Double, which is variegated with red and white shades; and the Chinese. The Double, however, is the most beautiful, and is composed of forty to fifty petals."

The Moors multiplied roses by all the various methods which are employed at this day: by suckers from the root, by cuttings, by budding, and by grafting. The pruning-knife was also freely used, in order to form regular heads.

There is a farther translation of De la Neuville from a Spanish version of the "Book of Agriculture," written by Ebu-Alwan, who lived in the twelfth century, and who, in addition to his own experience, quoted largely from some Chaldaic and Arabic writers. He states that the Moors practiced two methods of sowing the seeds of the Rose. The first was in earthen pans—a mode adapted to delicate plants; they were watered immediately after being sown, and afterward twice a week until autumn, when such care became unnecessary. The other method was sowing broadcast as grain is sown, then covering the seed-beds an inch deep with carefully sifted manure or fine mould, and giving them the requisite watering. The plants from these seed-beds did not produce flowers until the third year after their being thus prepared, and until they had been transplanted into squares or borders; such is still the case with nearly all our summer roses, the only kind the Moors appear to have possessed. They also understood the art of forcing roses. "If you wish," says Haj, another author, "the Rose tree to bloom in autumn, you must choose one that has been accustomed to periodical waterings; you must deprive it of water entirely during the heat of summer until August, and then give it an abundance of moisture; this will hasten its growth, and cause the expansion of its flowers in great profusion, without impairing its ability to bloom the ensuing spring, as usual." "Or else," adds the same author, "in the month of October, burn the old branches to the level of the earth, moisten the soil for eight consecutive days, and then suspend the watering; alternate these periods of moisture and drought as many as five times, and probably in about sixty days, or before the end of autumn, the roots will have thrown out vigorous branches, which will in due time be loaded with flowers, without destroying the ability of the plant to bloom again the following spring." The climate in which the Moors lived—that of Cordova, Grenada, and Seville, where the winter is very much like our weather in mid-autumn—was very favorable to the cultivation of the Rose. In this country the same results could doubtless be obtained in the Carolinas, and the experiment would be well worth trying, even in the latitude of New York. It would be no small triumph to obtain an autumnal bloom of the many beautiful varieties of French, Moss, or Provence Roses. Haj has also given the method of keeping the Rose in bud, in order to prolong its period of blooming. His process, however, is of so uncertain a character, as scarcely to merit an insertion here. The manuscript of De la Neuville also contains particular directions for propagating roses, and for planting hedges of the Eglantine, to protect the vineyards and gardens, and at the same time to serve as stocks for grafting. Nothing is omitted in the Arabian treatise which pertains to the management of this shrub; the manner of cultivating, weeding, transplanting, watering, etc., are all particularly explained. Among a variety of curious matters, it contains the process by which, for the purpose of embellishing their gardens, they produced the appearance of trees whose tops are loaded with roses. A hollow pipe, four feet long, or more, if the top was to be large, was obtained, of a well-proportioned diameter, set upright, to resemble the trunk of a tree, and filled with earth or sand in a suitable state of moisture. In the top of this pipe were planted several varieties of roses, of different colors, which, rooting freely in the earth around them, soon formed a bushy head, and represented a third-class tree, clothed with rich foliage and beautiful flowers.

This plan could now be practiced with success; and we can scarcely imagine more beautiful objects in a lawn than a number of these pipes, of various heights, single, and in groups, some low, with the small heads of the

China or Tea Roses, others high, and with the large, robust branches of the La Reine, and other Perpetuals, and others, again, planted with some delicate climbing roses, whose branches, falling down, would form a weeping tree of a most unique, graceful, and showy character. The pipes could be made of earthenware, tin, or wood, and be painted in imitation of the bark of a tree. Still better would be the trunk of a small tree, hollowed out for the purpose, which, with the bark on, would puzzle many a close observer, and which could show a luxuriant head of leaves and flowers on the most sterile soil that ever formed a lawn.

From what has been said on the culture of roses among the Moors in Spain, there can be no doubt that they had made great progress therein; and with the exception of a few statements, evidently unfounded in fact, as the grafting of the Rose on the almond, the apple, the jujube, and other trees, the little treatise translated by De la Neuville certainly contains most excellent remarks upon the culture of roses, whether we compare them with what the ancients have left us, or even with those of the various writers on Rose culture in Europe and America within the last half century.

As roses were so frequently propagated from the seed by the Moors, they must have known quite a number of varieties, exclusive of all those they had brought or obtained from the East. The Yellow Rose, unknown to us until recently, was apparently familiar to them; and the Blue Rose, of which their manuscripts speak, is now extinct, if it indeed ever existed; for amid the infinite variety of roses, of every color and shade, produced from seed in modern times, no one has yet obtained a purely Blue Rose, and its former existence may well seem to us incredible.

Besides the Moorish cultivation in Spain, the Rose has been an object of culture to a great extent in other countries. It has been cultivated principally for the beauty of its flowers, but in many parts of Europe and Asia, and in the north of Africa, its culture has been pursued for commercial purposes. Of its abundance in Palestine, some conception may be formed from the statement of travelers, that they have not only seen them wild and in great profusion in the vicinity of Jerusalem, but have found them in hedges, intermingled with pomegranate trees. Doubday states that, when the Eastern Christians made one of their processions in the Church of the Holy Sepulchre at Jerusalem, which continued some two hours, many persons were present with sacks full of rose petals, which they threw by handfuls on the people, and in such immense quantities, that many were covered with them, and they were scattered all over the pavement. In Syria and Persia it has been cultivated from a very early period, and the ancient name of the former, *Suristan*, is said to signify the land of roses. Damascus, Cashmere, Barbary, and Fayoum in Egypt, all cultivated the Rose extensively for its distilled oil or essence. Very little is extant respecting the culture of the Rose in the middle ages, but that it was cultivated and valued is known by its having been worn by knights at the tournament, as an emblem of their devotion to grace and beauty. According to Loudon, "Ludovico Verthema, who traveled in the East in 1503, observed that Tæssa was particularly celebrated for roses, and that he saw a great quantity of these flowers at Calicut." The Rose is to this day also extensively cultivated in India, and for commercial purposes perhaps in greater abundance than is now known in any other country. Bishop Heber states that "Ghazepoor is celebrated throughout India for the wholesomeness of its air and the beauty and extent of its rose gardens. The Rose-fields, which occupy many hundred acres in the neighborhood, are described as, at the proper season, extremely beautiful. They are cultivated for distillation and for making

'Attar of Roses.'" He states also, that "many roses were growing in the garden of the palace of Delhi, and the fountain pipes were carved with images of roses." Another writer describes in glowing colors the beauty of Ghazepoor, the Gul-istan (the rose beds,) of Bengal. "In the spring of the year, an extent of miles around the town presents to the eye a continual garden of roses, than which nothing can be more beautiful and fragrant. The sight is perfectly dazzling; the plain, as far as the eye can reach, extending in the same bespangled carpet of red and green. The breezes, too, are loaded with the sweet odor which is wafted far across the river Ganges."

These statements sufficiently evince that the Rose was not only valued by the Hindoos as an article of commerce, but was intimately associated with their ideas of pleasure and enjoyment.

Persia, however, was, above all other countries, preëminent for roses. "Sir John Chardin, in 1686, found the gardens of the Persians without parterres, labyrinths, and other ornaments of European gardens, but filled with lilies, peach trees, and roses; and all modern travelers bear testimony to the esteem in which this flower is held in the East." Sir Wm. Ousley tells us, in his travels in Persia, in 1819, that when he entered the flower garden belonging to the Governor of the Castle, near Farso, he was overwhelmed with roses; and Jackson, in his *Journey, etc.*, says that the roses of the Sinan Nile, or Garden of the Nile, are unequaled; and mattresses are made of their leaves, for men of rank to recline upon. Buckingham speaks of the rose plantations of Damascus as occupying an area of many acres, about three miles from that city. Sir Robert Ker Porter, speaking of the garden of one of the royal palaces of Persia, says: "I was struck with the appearance of two rose trees, full fourteen feet high, laden with thousands of flowers, in every degree of expansion, and of a bloom and delicacy of scent that imbued the whole atmosphere with exquisite perfume. Indeed, I believe that in no country in the world does the rose grow in such perfection as in Persia; in no country is it so cultivated and prized by the natives. Their gardens and courts are crowded by its plants, their rooms ornamented with roses, filled with its gathered branches, and every bath strewed with the full-blown flowers, plucked with the ever-replenished stems. * * * But in this delicious garden of Negaaristan, the eye and the smell are not the only senses regaled by the presence of the Rose: the ear is enchanted by the wild and beautiful notes of multitudes of nightingales, whose warblings seem to increase in melody and softness, with the unfolding of their favorite flowers. Here, indeed, the stranger is more powerfully reminded, that he is in the genuine country of the nightingale and the Rose." Rivers mentions that Sir John Malcolm told him, that when in Persia he had once breakfasted on an immense heap, or rather mount, of roses, which the Persians had raised in honor of him. The rose of Cashmere has been long celebrated in the East, for its brilliancy and delicacy of odor—

> "Who has not heard of the Vale of Cashmere,
> With its Roses, the brightest that earth ever gave?"

Throughout the whole season during which the roses remained in bloom in this beautiful valley, the Feast of Roses was kept with great rejoicing, and an entire abandonment to pleasure. At this time, a great number of tents were pitched, and multitudes of men, women, boys, and girls, were dancing and singing to the music of their various instruments.

All that has been handed down to us, and all we know at the present time of the climate and productions of Persia, and the customs of its inhabitants, prove that it was emphatically the land of roses; and all that we can gather from its history or tradition evinces, that to the inhabitants of the East, including the Hindoos and the Moors of Spain, is this beautiful flower indebted for the most careful and abundant cultivation, and for a due appreciation of its merits.

At the present time the Rose is cultivated throughout the civilized world. Loudon speaks of hedges of mixed Provence Roses, in the garden of Rosenstein, in Germany, and also of their profusion in the public garden of Frankfort. They are found in the gardens of Valencia, in Spain, and Sir John Carr, speaking of the seat of a Spanish gentleman near Tarragona, says, "The doors of the dining room open into a small garden, the walls of which are covered with myrtles, jasmines, and roses." In the Botanic garden of Madrid, rose trees are used for dividing hedges, and the flower is a favorite throughout Spain.

Among the Spanish ladies, the Rose is highly valued, and, with the Orange flower, is a favorite ornament for the hair. We have frequently been struck, while traveling in the Spanish West Indies, and in some parts of South America, with the careful nurture and attention bestowed on a single rose bush, and the delight exhibited at its bloom, while all around in natural luxuriance were the most beautiful and gorgeous plants and flowers which the tropics can produce. The brilliant cactus, the beautiful oleander, the singular orchids, and the delicate and fragrant flowers of the coffee and orange, seemed cast into the shade by the ancient and well-known Rose.

I well recollect, that on returning one day from a ride into the country, where I had been luxuriating in the gorgeous splendor of a tropical forest, the fair daughter of my hostess wished to introduce me to a flower, which, in her opinion, far surpassed all that I had seen; she accompanied me to the top of the flat-roofed house, used at the South as a place of evening resort, and there, in one corner, I found a thrifty plant of the Tea Rose, which to her infinite delight, was just showing above its glossy and delicate young leaves, a little ruby-tipped bud. This little plant had been the object of long and careful nursing, and her attention was now about to be rewarded by a fine and perfect bloom.

In France, however, is the Rose a preëminent object of horticulture, both in commercial establishments and in private gardens. The skill of the French has originated many new and beautiful varieties, which are to be found in several of the nurseries in the United States. The French are constantly searching for improvements in horticultural science and practice, with an enthusiasm rarely found in the more cold Englishman, whose skill seems to consist less in the creation of new varieties, than in growing perfectly those already known. None, indeed, can surpass the English in the art of growing fine plants, but we are chiefly indebted to the French for the finest new varieties of the Rose.

In Great Britain, although comparatively little attention has been paid to the obtaining of new varieties, the culture is more careful and the nomenclature more correct. The competition excited by their numerous horticultural exhibitions causes great attention to be given to correct nomenclature and to symmetrical habit of growth. We can imagine nothing more beautiful than some of the plants that we saw at the exhibitions of the London Horticultural Society at Chiswick; every plant was pruned, trained and grown, after an ideal, but perfect model, with its close and luxuriant foliage, its thrifty, symmetrical habit, and the thick, leathery petals of its well-cupped flower. This high standard should be introduced into every Society, and if such were the case in this country and the rule were carefully obeyed, the character of our exhibitions would in a short time be very materially changed.

T. Rivers is one of the most extensive rose cultivators in England, and is also known as the author of a very excellent descriptive work on the Rose. He has also been successful in hybridizing, and has originated some very fine varieties. His attention was at one time directed almost exclusively to the Rose, but it now includes many other nursery articles, and on our visit to him, we found him much interested with experiments in fruit culture. Lane, Wood, and Paul, are esteemed very good cultivators, and generally correct in their nomenclature. From these several establishments in England and France have been imported most of the varieties now existing in this country. Their trade with the United States is, however, comparatively limited, from the great risk of loss by a sea voyage. We have frequently lost in this way two-thirds or three-quarters of an importation, to our great annoyance and expense, and it is only by repeated and persevering importations that we have been able to obtain all the desirable varieties.

In the United States the culture of the Rose has been very much neglected, until within a few years. Tulips and dahlias have successively been the rage, and although there has long existed a great variety of roses, comparatively few of them have been cultivated, even in the best gardens of the United States. Now the tide is turning. Dahlias are going out of repute, and the Rose is resuming its ancient empire in the queendom of Flora. The advent of the Bourbon and the Remontant, or Perpetual classes, has no doubt materially aided this change, but it is in a great part owing to the easy culture of the plant, and the intrinsic merits and beauty of the flower. The taste of the horticultural public being thus decidedly for the Rose, a demand will exist for all the information respecting soil, planting, cultivating, etc., and this information we shall endeavor to supply in a simple and concise manner, avoiding, as far as possible, all technicalities, and adapting it to the use of the cultivator of a single plant in the crowded border of a city garden, or to the more extended culture of a commercial establishment.

Each cultivator has his peculiar mode of doing things, and there may be those who deem the mode laid down here inferior to their own. From these we should be glad to hear, and to make any corrections they may suggest, where such corrections appear to be founded upon true principles. In order to make our work as perfect as possible, we have not hesitated to add to our own experience all the information derived from a personal inspection of French and English nurseries, and to cull from foreign works and periodicals all that may interest our readers. Such information, as far as it coincides with our own experience, we shall gladly incorporate, with the hope that we may be successful in presenting every fact of interest which may exist respecting the cultivation of our favorite flower.

CHAPTER IV.

SOIL, SITUATION, AND PLANTING.

The most suitable soil is a strong, rich loam, or vegetable mould mixed with about one-quarter its bulk of well-decomposed stable manure. If the soil of the garden where the roses are to be planted differs materially from this, it should be made to approach it as nearly as possible by the addition of the requisite soil and manure. In a good vegetable garden, the soil, with the addition of a little manure, will grow the Rose well. When the soil, however, is of an inferior character, holes should be dug three or four times the size of the roots of a well-grown rose bush and filled with compost of the above character.

Rivers recommends, as the best compost for roses, rotten dung and pit-sand for cold, clayey soils; and for warm, dry soils, rotten dung and cool loams. He also states that he has found night soil, mixed with the drainings of the dunghill, or even with common ditch or pond water, so as to make a thick liquid, the best possible manure for roses, poured on the surface of the soil twice in winter—one to two gallons to each tree. The soil need not be stirred until spring, and then merely loosened two or three inches deep, with the prongs of a fork; for poor soil, and on lawns, previously removing the turf, this will be found most efficacious. He directs this compost to be applied in the first two winter months, but as our ground is frequently frozen so hard then that it cannot absorb the liquid, it would probably be best to apply it in this country a month earlier. Where a bed or border of roses is to be planted, it is well to dig out the soil to the depth of two or two and a half feet; fill the bottom to the depth of six inches with small stones, and then replace the earth, well fertilized, as directed above. Nothing is more injurious to the Rose than a wet, retentive subsoil; and where expense and trouble are no object, this perfect draining is much the best calculated to ensure a thrifty growth and perfect bloom. A rich and dry soil is, in fact, all-important; for otherwise the most double flower will frequently become single or semi-double. We have seen a plant of La Reine produce a perfect flower in the green-house, and when removed to an inferior soil, produce flowers almost single. It may therefore be safely laid down as a rule, that it is impossible to make the soil too rich for the Rose, and that in proportion to the fertilizing matter contained therein, provided it is properly decomposed, will be the approximation of the plant and the flower to perfection. The fertility of the soil may be very much assisted by frequent applications of liquid manure, made either of cow dung or guano; the former is always safe; the latter, valuable if properly used, may, in the hands of a careless person, ruin the plant.

In these remarks on fertility of soil, we have no desire to discourage those who may not have a fertile soil, or the means of obtaining the elements of fertility. The Rose will grow and bloom in any soil; the wood will be healthy, but short and small; the flower will be produced, but, as we have said before, will be smaller and often semi-double; yet even under these disadvantages, it is still the most desirable flower for the poor man; none other can so cheaply and so well ornament his small yard, or hanging in graceful festoons about his windows, shed forth its bloom and sweetness to enliven his hours of relief from labor, and give his children happiness, from the association of pleasant thought with natural beauty. But the poor man has within his reach more than he supposes of the elements of fertility. The ashes of his hearth, the decomposed turf of the road-side, and the domestic manure, too generally thrown away, all contain some of the best fertilizing matter, and with proper care could be made amply sufficient for the production of his flowers and vegetables. The decomposed turf alone would grow roses admirably, although a little manure would be a useful addition.

SITUATION.

The best situation for the Rose is an eastern or northern exposure, rather than a southern; the intensity of the heat of our midsummer often affects injuriously the expansion of the flowers, their color, and fragrance. A useful degree of shade can be obtained by planting amidst groups of dwarf roses, pillars, trellises, obelisks, etc., on which climbing roses can be trained, and whose shadow, changing with the sun, would protect the opening bloom and answer the same end as a cool situation. While, however, the Rose requires a cool, airy locality, it should by no means be placed entirely in the shade; a portion of the sun's rays is always necessary to ensure a good bloom. It is from this cause that the bloom of roses is much more certain and perfect in France and this country than in England. In the latter country, the sun is scarcely ever sufficiently powerful to develop all the resources of a plant. The summer of 1846 was unprecedentedly hot throughout England, and all the horticultural journals united in pronouncing the bloom of roses that season unsurpassed by the bloom of any previous year. For climbing roses the situation should not be too exposed, or where they would be liable to encounter heavy winds, which might break off the young shoots and in other ways injure the plant. Most of our American cities possess in the culture of roses a great advantage over the large towns of England, in the use of anthracite instead of bituminous coal; for, according to Loudon, the Rose will not thrive in towns where the prevailing fuel is of this character, and the bloom will not compare with those produced some ten miles distant. "The first effect of the smoke is to prevent the flower buds from opening freely, next to diminish their number; the leaves then gradually become smaller, and the length of the shoots less, after which the plant weakens by degrees, and in a few years, if a standard, it dies altogether, or, if a dwarf, barely exists, and seldom if ever flowers."

Such a result, from such a cause, is rarely known here, and the resident of the city may have his little yard filled with roses whose bloom will be in no way inferior to that of the plants in an extensive lawn or garden.

PLANTING.

All those roses that bloom only once in the year, and also the Perpetuals, or Remontant Roses, can be planted in autumn, after the first severe frost. The ends of the roots, which have been broken in taking up, will then form a callus, and the soil will be so thoroughly settled about the roots by the winter rains, that the plant will commence forming new roots early in the spring, and will rapidly make strong and luxuriant shoots. As far north as New York and its vicinity, the Bourbons and the Bengal, with their sub-classes, being more delicate, should not be planted until spring.

If the subsoil is wet and retentive of moisture, the planting of any roses should be deferred until spring, but from our preceding remarks it will be borne in mind that such soil should be well drained before planting, in which case the autumn will still answer.

The plant should be taken up carefully, with all the root possible, bearing in mind that the elements of life are in the root, and every fibre that is lost is so much taken from the future health and prosperity of the plant. The root should then be carefully examined, and every portion that has been bruised should be cut off; all the broken ends should also be cut away as far as they are split or injured. Any root of the character of a tap-root, or growing directly down into the earth, should be cut off; for it is best to encourage only lateral roots, which can more readily partake of the benefits of the rain and sun, and can more effectually absorb the nutriment in the soil.

In the spring the hole for each plant should be dug somewhat larger than the root, and the bottom forked, or dug up, and if necessary enriched with the surface soil, which, it is presumed, has been prepared according to preceding directions. Let one hold the plant, while another throws in the soil; or if one alone is planting, let him hold the stem just above the root with one hand, and throw in the soil with the other, moving the stem from side to side, and occasionally pulling it upward a little and shaking the root until the soil has worked well among the fibres; on which much of the subsequent prosperity of the plant depends. If the weather is dry, a little water may be placed in the hole, which should then be filled up and the soil well trodden down about the stem. When planted, it should be very little, if at all, lower in the ground than before; very little of the stem should be buried; and when trodden down, the root should be made firm and solid.

In planting climbing or pillar roses, care should be taken to set the trellis, or pillar, or whatever may be used for their support, before the plant is put in the ground; for if such should be set after the plant has commenced growing vigorously, it will in all probability damage the roots, and give the plant a check from which it will not recover during the whole season.

The Rose, even in the best soils, should be taken up every three or four years, and have its roots shortened and pruned; a portion of the soil in which it grew should also be removed and replaced by soil of the character before described. Where the soil is poor, they should be taken up every other year, and replanted, after renewing the soil as above, or digging it with plenty of manure.

Van Mons states that in Belgium the plants are uniformly taken up at the end of eight years and placed in fresh soil, or they are thrown away and young plants substituted in their place. This substitution of young plants is perhaps the most certain mode of ensuring a continual supply of strong, healthy wood and well-formed flowers.

The Rose may be transplanted at any season, provided the shoots are pruned closely and deprived of all their leaves, and the soil in which they are planted kept well watered. The flowering also may be retarded in this way, and those roses that bloom only once in the season, if they are transplanted just before they are coming into flower, and properly pruned, will bloom in autumn. The autumn and spring, or the dormant season, however, is the proper period for all transplanting.

Whether planted in autumn or spring, if purchased of a nurseryman, they should be *ordered* in the autumn. In the spring, as soon as the frost is out of the ground, the first few warm days, operating upon their excitable nature, will start them into growth. If then the nurseryman has a large number of orders on hand, some of them will inevitably be delayed until the plants have grown too much. If ordered in the autumn, the purchaser should not expect to receive them before the 10th or 15th of November. No nurseryman who values his reputation will allow roses to leave his grounds before the vegetation is checked by several heavy frosts, and the wood and roots allowed time thereafter to thoroughly ripen. Dealers who desire roses early, in order to deliver with other plants, sometimes rebel at this; but purchasers should understand that roses will not flourish unless the wood and roots are thoroughly ripe. This applies more particularly to the Remontant,

Moss, and June roses. The Tea, China, and Noisette, will bear taking up at any time, but their roots will rarely be in a condition to endure the cold as far north as New York without some protection. When received from the nurseryman in the autumn, they should be carefully and separately heeled-in in a dry piece of land, and covered with sand. A covering of litter should be avoided, because it affords a harbor for mice, who would soon destroy the plants.

Plants from the open ground are always to be preferred by the purchaser. Those sold in pots in the spring have frequently been forced, and will require a long period of rest before growing again, while those from the open ground, having had their rest, will grow luxuriantly at once.

It should also be remembered by the purchaser that the delicate roots of the Rose will not bear exposure to the air. All reputable nurserymen understand this, and pack in moss. Dealers, however, who purchase of these nurserymen, and who have many lots to deliver after they are unpacked, are often not sufficiently careful to guard the roots against exposure. The plants then failing to grow well, the fault is attributed to some deficiency in the plant, rather than to its true cause. To ensure safety while being delivered, dealers should dip them, as soon as unpacked, in a puddle of mud of the consistency of thick paint. This precaution is useful in every case after unpacking and before planting, for there must always be some delay and exposure even when the purchaser obtains plants directly from the grower.

CHAPTER V.

PRUNING, TRAINING, AND BEDDING.

In pruning roses at the time of transplanting, the principal object to be attained is relief to the plant by taking away all the wood and branches which the diminished root may not be able to support. The mode of pruning depends very much upon the condition of the plant. If it is very bushy, all the weaker branches should be cut away, leaving not more than three or four of the strongest shoots, and shortening even those down to a few eyes. If it is desired that the plant should continue dwarf and bushy, the new wood should be cut down to the lower two eyes, and every half-grown or slender shoot cut out. These two eyes will each throw out a branch; then cut these branches down to the two eyes, and again cut back the shoots they produce until a symmetrical habit is formed, with close, thick foliage. There should not be sufficient wood allowed to remain to make the bush crowded; and if there should be danger of this, some of the branches, instead of being cut down to two eyes, should be removed altogether.

Climbing roses, when planted, should be cut down almost to the ground, and also carefully thinned out. Only a few of the strongest branches should be preserved, and the new wood of these cut down to two eyes each.

The preceding remarks are applicable to roses at the time of planting; they should also be pruned every year, —the hardy varieties in the autumn or winter, and the more tender in the spring. For all roses that are not liable to have part of their wood killed by the cold, the autumn is decidedly the best time for pruning; the root, having then but little top to support, is left at liberty to store up nutriment for a strong growth the following season. The principal objects in pruning are the removal of the old wood, because it is generally only the young wood that produces large and fine flowers; the shortening and thinning out of the young wood, that the root, having much less wood to support, may devote all its nutriment to the size and beauty of the flower; and the formation of a symmetrical shape. If an abundant bloom is desired, without regard to the size of the flower, only the weak shoots should be cut out, and the strong wood should be shortened very little; each bud will then produce a flower. By this mode, the flowers will be small, and the growth of new wood very short, but there will be an abundant and very showy bloom. If, however, the flowers are desired as large and as perfect as possible, all the weak wood should be cut out entirely, and all the strong wood formed the last season should be cut down to two eyes. The knife should always be applied directly above a bud, and sloping upward from it. The preceding observations apply principally to rose bushes, or dwarf roses; with pillar, climbing, and tree roses, the practice should be somewhat different. The former two need comparatively little pruning; they require careful thinning out, but should seldom be shortened. The very young side shoots can sometimes be shortened in, to prevent the foliage from becoming too thick and crowded.

Pillars for roses can be made of trellis work, of iron rods in different forms, or of wood, but they should enclose a space of at least a foot in diameter. The cheapest plan, and one that will last many years, is to make posts of about 1½ or 2 inches square, out of locust or pitch-pine plank, and connect them with common hoop-iron. They should be the length of a plank—between twelve and thirteen feet—and should be set three feet in the ground, that they may effectually resist the action of the wind. The Rose having been cut down to the ground, is planted inside of the pillar, and will make strong growths the first season. As the leading shoots appear, they should be trained spirally around the outside of the pillar, and sufficiently near each other to enable them to fill up the intermediate space with their foliage. These leading shoots will then form the permanent wood, and the young side shoots, pruned in from year to year, will produce the flowers, and at the flowering season cover the whole pil-

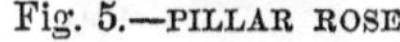

Fig. 5.—PILLAR ROSE.

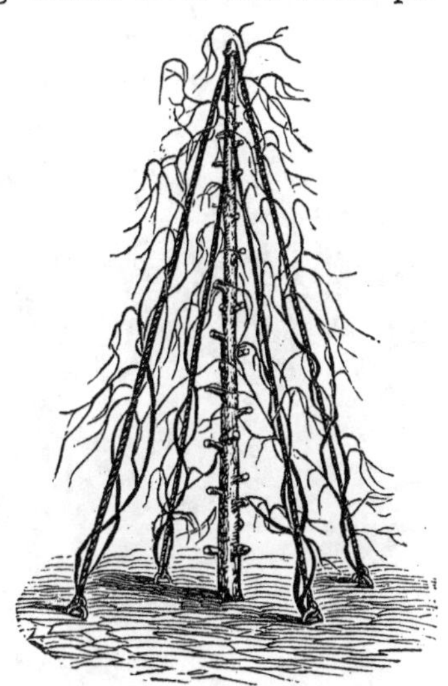

Fig. 6.—ROSE PYRAMID.

lar with a mass of rich and showy bloom. Figure 5 gives the appearance of a pillar of this kind. If the tops of the leading shoots die down at all, they should be shortened down to the first strong eye, because, if a weak bud is left at the top, its growth will be slender for a long time. The growth of different varieties of roses is very varied; some make delicate shoots, and require little room, while others, like the Queen of the Prairies, are exceedingly robust, and may require a larger pillar than the size we have mentioned. Figure 6 shows the method of constructing a pyramid by the use of a central post and iron rods.

Climbing roses require very much the same treatment as pillar roses, and are frequently trained over arches, or in festoons from one pillar to another. In these the weak branches should also be thinned out, and the strong ones be allowed to remain, without being shortened, as in these an abundant bloom is wanted, rather than large flowers. An arbor, made by training roses from one pillar to another, is represented in figure 7. In training climbing

Fig. 7.—A ROSE ARBOR.

roses over any flat surface, as a trellis, wall, or side of a house, the principal point is so to place the leading shoots that all the intermediate space may be filled up with foliage. They can either be trained in fan-shape, with side shoots growing out from a main stem, or one leading shoot can be encouraged and trained in parallel horizontal lines to the top, care being taken to preserve sufficient intermediate space for the foliage. Where no shoots are wanted, the buds can be rubbed off before they push out. No weak shoots should be allowed to grow from the bottom, but all the strong ones should be allowed to grow as much as they may. When the intermediate space is filled with young wood and foliage, all the thin, small shoots should be cut out every year, and the strongest buds only allowed to remain, which, forming strong branches, will set closely to the wall and preserve a neat appearance.

The production of roses out of season, by forcing, was, as we have shown, well known to the ancient Romans, and from them has been handed down to the present time. But the retarding of roses by means of a regular process of pruning owes its origin to a comparatively modern date. This process is mentioned both by Lord Bacon and Sir Robert Boyle. The latter says: "It is delivered by the *Lord Verulam*, and other naturalists, that if a rose bush be carefully cut as soon as it is done bearing in the summer, it will again bear roses in the autumn. Of this, many have made unsuccessful trials, and thereupon report the affirmation to be false; yet I am very apt to think that my lord was encouraged by experience to write as he did. For, having been particularly solicitous about the experiment, I find by the relation, both of my own and other experienced gardeners, that this way of procuring autumnal roses will, in most rose bushes, commonly fail, but succeed in some that are good bearers; and, accordingly, having this summer made trial of it, I find that of a row of bushes cut in June, by far the greater number promise no autumnal roses; but one that hath manifested itself to be of a vigorous and prolific nature is, at this present, indifferently well stored with those of the damask kind. There may, also, be a mistake in the species of roses; for experienced gardeners inform me that the Musk Rose will, if it be a lusty plant, bear flowers in autumn without cutting; and, therefore, that may unjustly be ascribed to art, which is the bare production of nature." Thus, in quaint and ancient style, discourses the wise and pious philosopher on our favorite flower, and also mentions the fact, that a *red* rose becomes *white* on being exposed to the fumes of sulphur. This, however, had been observed before Sir Robert's time. Notwithstanding his doubts, it is now a well-established fact, that the blooming of roses may be retarded by cutting them back to two eyes after they have fairly commenced growing, and the flower buds are discoverable. A constant succession can be obtained where there is a number of plants, by cutting each one back a shorter or longer distance, or at various periods of its growth. In these cases, however, it very often will not bloom until autumn, because the second effort to produce flowers is much greater than the first, and is not attended with success until late in the season.

However desirable may be this retarding process, it cannot be relied on as a general practice, because the very unusual exertion made to produce the flowers a second time, weakens the plant, and materially affects its prosperity the subsequent year.

There is, indeed, but one kind of summer pruning that is advantageous, which is the thinning out of the flower-buds as soon as they appear, in order that the plant may be burdened with no more than it can fully perfect, and the cutting off all the seed vessels after the flower has expanded and the petals have fallen. Until this last is done, a second bloom cannot readily be obtained from the Bengal Rose and its sub-classes, the Tea and Noisette, which otherwise grow and bloom constantly throughout the season.

We would impress upon our readers the absolute, the essential, importance of cultivation—of constantly stirring the soil in which the Rose is planted; and we scarcely know of more comprehensive directions in a few words than the reply of an experienced horticulturist to one who asked the best mode of growing fine fruits and flowers. The old gentleman replied that the mode could be described in three words, "cultivate, cultivate, cultivate." After the same manner, we would impress the importance of these three words upon all those who love well-grown and beautiful roses. They are, indeed, *multum in parvo* —the very essence of successful culture. The soil cannot be plowed, dug, or stirred too much; it should be dug and hoed, not merely to keep down the weeds, but to ensure the health and prosperity of the plant. Cultivation is to all plants and trees manure, sun, and rain. It opens the soil to the nutrition it may receive from the atmosphere, to the beneficial influence of light, and to the morning and evening dew. It makes the heavy soil light, and the light soil heavy; if the earth is saturated with rain, it dries it; if burned up with drought, it moistens it. Watering is often beneficial, and is particularly so to roses just before and during the period of bloom; but in an extremely dry season, if we were obliged to choose between the watering-pot and the spade, we should most unhesitatingly give the preference to the latter.

We do not wish, however, to undervalue the benefits of water. If the plants are well mulched with straw, salt hay, or any other litter, frequent watering is very beneficial. When not mulched, the watering should always be followed by the hoe, in order to destroy the baking of the surface. While the plants are in a growing state, liquid manure will give a larger and a finer bloom. This liquid manure may be made with soapsuds, or the refuse from the house. When these are not easily obtained, half a bushel of cow or horse dung can be placed in a barrel, which can then be filled with water, well stirred up, and allowed to settle a day or two before being used.

For those who are willing to incur the expense, a very nice way of applying pure water is to sink ordinary tile, two inches in diameter, with collars, about a foot below the surface, around and through the rose bed. An elbow from this, coming to the surface, can convey the water into the pipes, through the joints of which it will escape, and thus irrigate the whole ground, without baking the surface.

BEDDING ROSES.

While Remontant, Moss, and Garden Roses are adapted to the wants of much the larger number of growers, because they require no protection in winter, and are strong and robust in their growth and habit, yet the everblooming varieties are becoming daily more popular. While but few of the Remontants have more than two seasons of distinct and abundant bloom, the Teas, Chinas, and Noisettes, bloom constantly and continuously. In grace, and color, and beauty, these last have more varied charms than the more hardy and abundant Remontants, and the difficulty of caring for them in the winter, even by those who have no glass, is compensated by the additional pleasure they give in the summer. Those who have glass can enjoy them winter and summer alike. Their superiority in constant blooming, especially, adapts them for planting in masses or beds scattered about the lawn. These beds can be each of one color, or they can be assorted, or can be planted in the ribbon style, rows of white, or red, or yellow alternating. No bedding flowers, Verbenas, Salvias, or any other plant, will give so constant pleasure as Roses. They can be purchased, also, nearly as cheaply as ordinary bedding plants, and are found in several places as low as $15 per 100, or $100 per 1,000. On being taken out of the pots they will grow rapidly, and bloom after they are thoroughly established, and afterward, year after year, they will commence blooming early, and continue until frost. A bed made in any part of the lawn, and in any soil, will grow them well, provided it has a dry bottom, and has some well-decomposed manure dug in it. A light, sandy soil will grow them in the greatest perfection. They can be planted eighteen inches to two feet apart, and the new shoots, as soon as they have attained sufficient length, should be pegged down, so as to cover the whole ground. The branches thus laid down will give abundant flowers throughout their whole length, and from each bud a strong-rooted shoot will be thrown up, and being pruned down close in the autumn, will be ready to produce a strong and bearing shoot another year. If they become too close and crowded, the new shoots can be partially cut away. North of Baltimore, these Roses will need protection in the winter. This can be done by covering the bed with sand, several inches deep, or by taking up the plants, cutting them down, heeling them in in a dry cellar, or potting them for a green-house.

CHAPTER VI.

POTTING AND FORCING.

"Seek Roses in December, ice in June."—BYRON.

Every variety of Rose, in the hands of a skillful man, will grow and bloom well in pots, although the Bengal and its sub-classes, and the more dwarf Hardy Roses, are the most easily managed. The great point in potting is to imitate planting in the open ground as nearly as possible. The soil used should possess all the nutritious elements required in the open ground, and, if possible, in somewhat greater abundance. More manure should be used, because the frequent watering required by plants in pots must inevitably wash away a portion of the fertilizing matter. There is nothing better than one portion of stable manure, and three of turf, or leaf-mould, all well decomposed, and mixed with a little pure peat earth. A portion of night-soil, well incorporated with charcoal, is also very excellent. Charcoal is the most powerful absorbent known; it retains the nutritious elements in the night-soil, prevents their being washed away by watering, and gives them out as the plant needs them. English gardeners should bear in mind that roses require in this climate a stronger soil than in England. Half-gallon pots are the best size at first, from which, by repeated pottings, corresponding with the growth of the plant, they can be shifted to one or two-gallon pots. The size of the pots should, however, be regulated by the extent of the roots; it should be just sufficiently large to allow the roots to go in without crowding. A few broken pieces of pots or small lumps should be put in the bottom for drainage. When the plant is to be taken from the open ground, select one, the roots of which are not too large, and with a sharp spade cut around it a ball of earth about the size of the pot, depriving it at the same time of a portion of its top, as directed in remarks on pruning. It should stand in this state about a fortnight, until the roots have become callused, and the plant is somewhat accustomed to the loss of its roots and branches. It can then be safely taken up at any season, and transferred to the pot, which should then be filled in with earth, firm and solid. If potted in the autumn, after the leaves have fallen and the wood become mature, the above previous preparation is not required, but the plant can be taken up without a ball of earth, and after being pruned of its bruised or broken roots, placed in the pot. It should then be protected from the frost and light until it has entirely recovered from its change of habitation, when it can be placed in any cool spot free from frost, until it is wanted for forcing.

Roses may, without difficulty, by the above previous management, be forced to bloom in the latter part of winter, but where their bloom is desired at Christmas or New-Year, they should be gradually prepared for the space of a year previous. To produce roses the latter part of winter, our own management has been simple and effective, giving us as many flowers as a green-house and vinery full of pots could afford. After putting the plants in pots, as directed above, pruning them down to eight or ten buds, and hardening them in a shady place, they are removed to the vinery before the frost out of doors can have injured them, and cut down to two buds. The house is then kept as cool as possible, while the frost is carefully excluded by a light fire at night, and on fine days the sashes are opened, and plenty of air admitted. They are thus kept in a dormant state until the first of the year, when the heat is gradually increased to about 70° by day, sinking as low as 35° at night. Care is taken to give them sufficient watering, and in their whole management to subject them as nearly as possible to the conditions of open culture. When the green-fly appears, it is immediately destroyed by fumigation with tobacco, and the plants are subsequently syringed with clean water. With this management, they soon begin to show signs of life, the bud commences pushing forth its delicate, light green shoot, the leaves then appear, the plant, soon growing with luxuriance, is clothed with rich foliage, and about the middle of the third month, the house presents a mass of thrifty growth and perfect bloom.

By the means above described, roses may be forced into bloom the latter part of winter; and by observing some care to bring them into the house at different periods, in regular succession, a bloom can be enjoyed through all the spring months, until roses bloom in the open ground. This process cannot, however, be continued two years in succession without weakening the plant; and although, if placed in a shady spot, and allowed to rest during the summer, it may sufficiently recover to perform the same work another year, it is desirable, if possible, to have fresh plants, whose strength has not been exhausted by the unusual effort attending the production of flowers out of season.

The preceding directions apply more particularly to late forcing; and although the same means, with an earlier application of heat, will produce flowers early in winter, yet the true art of early forcing consists in *gradually* bringing the Rose out of its season; and it is only by this mode that thrifty plants and perfect flowers can be produced before Christmas.

Two years, and sometimes three, should be employed in preparing a Rose for early forcing. Having been prepared by digging around it with a sharp spade some two weeks previously, the plant should be taken up immediately after the first frost, placed in a cold frame a few days, to harden, and then taken to the green-house or vinery. A moderate heat should then be given it, with plenty of light and air to prevent its being drawn. The flower-buds should be plucked off as soon as they appear, and no bloom should be allowed. It will thus make fine growths, and can be plunged in the open ground as soon as danger of frost has passed in the spring. Here it can remain during the summer, to ripen its wood, and will require no care except a little watering in dry weather, and an occasional taking up and examination, that the roots may not push through the hole of the pot, and become fixed in the ground, in which case the plants would make too strong a growth, and suffer on being removed from the new-made root. In October it can be placed in a pot one size larger, pruned by thinning out all the weak branches, and shortening the strong ones down to two eyes. It should then go through the same process as before, carefully picking off all the flower-buds, promoting its growth until completed, when let it be put in a cold frame until all danger of frost is over, and then plunge it in the ground to ripen its wood. As its vegetation was started a month earlier the last year, it can now be taken up in September, repotted and pruned as before, and then taken into the green-house. The temperature should then be gradually raised to about 55° until the plant has commenced growing, and then gradually increased to 65° or 70°, giving as much air as can be obtained without lowering the temperature.

All useless shoots should be kept down, and all the flower-buds taken off that threaten to be abortive. In fumigating for the green-fly, care should be taken not to do it too strongly, but repeated and gentle doses at night are better. We have known many fine plants ruined by fumigation in the hands of an inexperienced person. A good bloom can be obtained the second year by this mode; but if the amateur has the patience to wait until a third, he will be rewarded by a thrifty and compact habit, rich foliage, and beautiful bloom for two months before Christmas; and if there are a number of plants to be brought into the green-house a week after each other, he can have them in bloom until the late forced roses appear. At all periods subsequent to their commencement, care should be taken to give them sufficient moisture, and as much air as is consistent with the state of growth and the external temperature. Without water, they will neither grow nor bloom well. Under glass, every other day, and in some cases, twice a week is sufficient.

The great principle to be borne in mind in forcing roses is, that sudden excitement is fatal, and that a plant should never be taken from the open ground into a heated house without being gradually prepared for it. This principle is particularly applicable to deciduous roses. The Remontant and Bourbon, the Bengal and its sub-classes, which grow and bloom through the whole year, are not so liable to be injured by exciting treatment.

Cuttings of these that are struck in the spring and planted out in the open ground may have their tops slightly pruned, and their buds all pinched off during the summer, to encourage the formation of wood and of a close head.

About the last days of summer, or the first of autumn, they can be taken up and placed in quart pots, with a soil composed of one half loam, one quarter cow-dung, and one quarter peat. After being slightly pruned, and left in the shade for a week, they can be placed in frames, protected at night from frost, and exposed to the air in mild weather for some two months, when they can be removed, a few at a time, into the green-house, and subjected to a moderately increased temperature. They will soon bloom well, and will succeed each other throughout the winter and spring, until roses bloom in the open air. Like the deciduous roses, they require to be protected against the green-fly by syringing, and if that does not answer, by fumigation with tobacco.

The Bengal, however, like the deciduous roses, will bloom better the second winter than the first, by shifting them into larger pots, pruning them, cutting off all the flower-buds, and giving them very little water the latter part of summer. They can then be put into the frames, and treated as before. The Bengal Rose is very easily forced in this way; and if the temperature is at first kept during the day at 45°, and gradually increased to 60°, there can be little difficulty in obtaining beautiful and healthy plants. This temperature can be obtained in any green-house or vinery. The latter is becoming more common, and when it is provided with heating apparatus, there can be nothing better for roses. We have forced them very successfully in one of our own vineries, one hundred and twenty feet long, twelve feet wide, ten feet high in the rear, three and a half in front, and heated by hot water. But as there may be many who desire a cheaper structure, we will give the description of one used by Rivers, (the best rose-grower known), with his mode of managing roses in a structure of that character. "A pit, ten or twelve feet long, and eight feet wide, just high enough to stand upright in, with a door at one end, and a sunken path in the centre, a raised bed on each side of the path, and an 18-inch Arnott's stove at the farther end, opposite to the door, with a pipe leading into a small brick chimney outside, (a chimney is indispensable), will give a great abundance of forced roses from February to the end of May. To ensure this, a supply must be kept ready, so that, say twenty may be placed in the forcing pit about the middle of December, a like number in the middle of January, and the same about the middle of February; they must not be pruned till taken into the house, when each shoot should be cut back to two or three buds for the formation of strong shoots. The fire should be lighted at seven in the morning, and suffered to burn out about the same hour in the evening, unless in frosty weather, when it must be kept burning till late at night, so as to exclude the frost; and for this purpose, double mats should be placed on the lights. The thermometer should not, by *fire heat*, be higher in the day than 70° during December, January, and February; at night it may sink to 35° without injury. The temporary rise in a sunny day is of no consequence, but *no air must be admitted at such times, or the plants will exhaust themselves, and immediately shed their leaves.* When the sun begins to have power, and in sunny weather, toward the end of February, the plants may be syringed every morning about 10 o'clock with tepid water, and smoked with tobacco at night on the least appearance of the Aphis, or green-fly. To ensure a fine and full crop of flowers, the plants should be established one year in pots, and plunged in tan or sawdust, in an open, exposed place, that their shoots may be well ripened; the pots must be often removed, or, what is better, place the pots on slates, to prevent their roots striking into the ground. With the Remontant or Perpetuals, even if only potted in November previous, a very good crop of flowers may often be obtained, and a second crop better than the first; for the great advantage of forcing Remontant roses is, that after blooming in the green-house or drawing-room, their young shoots may be cut down to within two or three buds of their base, and the plants placed again in the forcing-house, and a second crop of flowers obtained. The same mode may be followed also with the Bourbon, China, and Tea-scented roses; with the latter, indeed, a third crop may be often obtained. Toward the end of March, when the second crop of flowers is coming on, the plants may be gradually inured to the air, by opening the sashes in mild weather. This will make them hardy and robust. Syringing should be practiced every morning and evening; but when the flower-buds are ready to open, this must be confined to the stems of the plants and the pots; otherwise the flowers will be injured by the moisture. Air must at first only be given about noon; care must be taken to remove the plants from the forcing-house to the green-house or drawing-room before their blossoms expand; they may then be kept in beauty many days. We have not found the check which the plants receive by this sudden change of temperature at all detrimental. During their second growth, the plants should be watered once a week with manure-water, and the surface of the pot occasionally stirred. Two pounds of guano to ten gallons of water forms the very best species of liquid manure; this should be stirred before it is used.

"The treatment recommended for roses in a pit with Arnott's stove may be pursued with roses in a house with smoke-flues or hot-water pipes. Arnott's stove is recommended as an economical and eligible mode of heating, practiced here to some extent with success for several years. On these stoves an iron pan, fitted to the top, should always be kept full of water. Roses may be forced slowly, but with perhaps greater certainty by the uninitiated, by giving air freely and constantly in mild weather during the day, keeping the fire constantly burning during the same period, as recommended when keeping them closely shut up."

We have copied the whole of this article, although in a measure a repetition of previous remarks, since it may be interesting to some to know the opinion of so eminent a cultivator on this least understood branch of rose culture. A few of his directions are somewhat different from those we have given before, and may be far better than our own plan, in the climate of England. Here, an Arnott's stove would scarcely heat a pit to 70° with the thermometer at zero; and if it should, we would think it rather dangerous to give so high a temperature at once.

The strength of guano is also so varied, that we should feel very cautious in using it according to the above receipt. While, however, we would not venture to question the general utility of his directions, we may perhaps say, that we have found our own plan effective in its results, and productive of thrifty plants and beautiful flowers. We would advise cultivators to test them both, and adopt that which succeeds best in their hands. A pit of the above description can be constructed at a very low price, and should be found on the premises of every gentleman of even very moderate income, for the supply of his parlors during winter. If, in addition to this, there were constructed on the east side of the house, and facing south, a little room with a glass front and roof, opening into the parlor, and heated either by a valve from the house furnace, or by a water-back connected with the parlor grate, more enjoyment would be afforded the lover of flowers than could be obtained by any other outlay of two hundred dollars. This room could then be kept constantly filled with roses from the pit, and through the most dreary winter, amid rain, snow, and storm, would present a bright array of the living reminders of spring and summer. It is a matter of much surprise, that, among all the beautiful country residences in the vicinity of our large cities, surrounded by all the appliances of luxury and comfort that taste and wealth can afford, so few instances are found in which the drawing-room or parlor opens into a green-house or conservatory. These buildings are frequently placed at a distance from the house, and although they may be filled with the most beautiful and rare exotics, are, during the greater part of the winter, inaccessible to the ladies of the family.

Let gentlemen of wealth, then, place their vineries anywhere, but use them as forcing-houses when the vines are in a dormant state. Let them also have a green-house or conservatory opening from the drawing-room, into which all the plants can be brought from the vinery whenever they show signs of bloom. This conservatory can be heated by hot water, flowing through iron pipes from a boiler placed over the furnace that warms the drawing-room—taking from this very little heat, and yet abundantly warming the conservatory. An improvement could still farther be made, by having the east end of the conservatory arch over a carriage drive, and thus allow visitors to enter the drawing-room through the conservatory. Exclusive of the delight afforded visitors by this very pleasant addition to a dwelling, it affords a delightful promenade for the ladies of the family, where, while all is wintry without, and walking is unpleasant, even when the ice-bound trees are glittering in the clear sunlight, they may luxuriate amid roses and jasmines, breathing air fragrant with the perfume of daphne and orange flowers, and surrounded with everything that can remind them of the beauty and bland climate of the sunny south.

We have occupied so much space with the peculiarities of culture for the forcing-house, that we had almost forgotten that more humble, but no less pleasure-giving mode of Window culture. As this culture is practiced chiefly by those who cannot spare the time nor incur the expense of previous preparation, the best mode is that given for late forcing of roses, taken up the autumn previous, placing the plants in pots seven inches in diameter, and using a soil composed of equal parts of sand, loam, and manure, or peat, loam, and manure. They can be watered with manure-water every fortnight, made from the drippings of the barn-yard, or, what is more pleasant, a safely weak solution of guano, about one pound to fifteen gallons.

The plants should be brought into the heat gradually; first into a cold room where there is no frost, and then into the sitting-room, where they can be placed in the window, and turned around every week, in order to give each side of the plant its share of light. They will soon begin to put forth their thrifty shoots, in some six weeks will present a fine show of beautiful flowers, and, if properly managed, will continue blooming through the winter. If attacked by the green-fly, the plant can be inverted in a strong decoction of tobacco, or it can be fumigated by being placed under an inverted barrel, or other receptacle, with some burning tobacco. For window culture, the Everblooming Roses are the best, and they should be ordered of the nurseryman in suitable pots. This mode commends itself to all; it is within the reach of the daily laborer; the seamstress can have it in her window, and in the midst of her toilsome duties, be reminded by its bright flowers of many a green spot in past days. It is especially suited to the means and leisure of the operatives in our factories, many of whom have left the country and all its green fields and pleasant flowers for the crowded city, where they can have no garden, but simply this little pot to remind them of past pleasures, and throw a gleam of sunshine over their hours of relief from labor. The plant can be placed in their chamber window, or in the windows of the factory, where the high temperature, if it has been brought from the chamber, will soon bring out its foliage in great luxuriance, and its flowers in beauty, and be a pleasant object of care in the moments snatched from the operations of the loom. To this class we would especially commend the Rose; as thriving under simple treatment, as possessing, more than any other flower, the elements of beauty, and tending, like other flowers, to keep alive in a crowded city that freshness and purity of feeling that distinguished their country life, and which, unless there exists an unusual perversion of the moral faculties, must always result from an intimate acquaintance with natural objects.

CHAPTER VII.

PROPAGATION OF THE ROSE.

CUTTINGS.

This mode of propagation, although possible with all roses, is more difficult with those that bloom only once in the season. It is most applicable to the smooth-wooded kinds, as the Bengal and its sub-classes, and the Boursault, Microphylla, rubifolia, etc. Many of the Perpetuals and Bourbons are propagated with facility by the same mode. For propagation in the open ground, cuttings should be made in the autumn, or early part of winter. They should be made of wood of the growth of the season, and about six inches long. The lower end should be cut square, close to a bud, and they can then be planted thickly, two-thirds of their length in sand, in a light and dry cellar. Here a callus will be formed on the bottom of each cutting during the winter, and on being planted out in the spring, they will immediately throw out roots. They should be planted as early as possible in the spring, in a light sandy loam, with one-third of their length and at least one bud above the surface of the ground. They should be planted very early in the spring, because, if left until late, the power of the sun is too much for them. The earth should be trodden down very tight about them, in order, as much as possible, to exclude the air. If the weather is dry, they should be carefully watered in the evening. Where it is inconvenient to make the cuttings in the fall or early in the winter, they can be made in the spring; but in consequence of having to form the callus, they will require a much lighter soil than will afterward be desirable for their growth, and they will also be much later in coming on. This mode of open propagation answers very well for some of the smooth-wooded roses of the more robust growing varieties, like the Boursault and Rubifolia; but for the delicate Bengals, the best mode is pot propagation. For this purpose, small pots can be used, filled with equal parts of mould and sand, or peat and sand. About the middle of autumn, cuttings of the same season's growth are taken off with two to four buds, cutting off one or two of the lower leaves, and cutting off the wood smooth and square close to the eye, as in figure 8. These cuttings can be inserted in the pot, leaving one eye above the surface. It should then be slightly watered to settle the soil firmly around the cuttings, and then placed in a cold frame, or on the floor of a vinery, in which no fire is kept during winter. Early in the spring the pot should be placed in a house with a moderate temperature, kept perfectly close, and sprinkled every morning with water a little tepid. Now, as well as during the autumn, they should be shaded from the too bright glare of the sun. In about a fortnight, and after they have formed a third set of leaves and good roots, a little air can be given them; and after being thus hardened for a week, they can be repotted into larger pots. In order to ascertain when they are sufficiently rooted, the ball of earth can be taken out of the pot, by striking its inverted edge lightly against some body, at the same time sustaining the ball of earth

Fig. 8.—A ROSE CUTTING.

by the hand, the cutting being passed between two of the fingers a little separated. If well rooted, the fibres will be seen on the outside of the ball of earth. They can then be placed in a cold frame, or anywhere under glass, to be planted out the latter part of spring, or retained for pot culture. Where hot-bed frames are not convenient, or the amateur wishes only to experiment with one or two cuttings, he can use a tumbler, or any kind of close glass covering.

Where roses are forced into bloom the latter part of winter, cuttings can be taken from them immediately after the bloom is past; and they will also succeed if taken from plants in the open ground immediately after their first bloom. Cuttings of the Everblooming Roses will all strike at any time during the summer, but they succeed much better either in the autumn, or after their first bloom. The heat of our midsummer sun is so great upon plants forced in the house, that cuttings often fail at that time. When a cutting is made near the old stem, it is better to take with it a portion of the old wood, which forms the enlarged part of the young branch. Where the cuttings are scarce, two buds will answer very well—one below the surface; and, in some cases, propagation has been successful with only one eye. In this case they are planted up to the base of the leaf in pots of sand, similar to that used in the manufacture of glass, and the eye is partially covered. They are then subject to the same treatment as the others, and carefully shaded; they will thus root easily, but require a long time to make strong plants.

Some years since, Lecoq, a French cultivator, conceived the idea of endeavoring to propagate roses by the leaf. He gathered some very young leaves of the Bengal rose, about one quarter developed, cutting them off at their insertion, or at the surface of the bark. He planted these in peat soil, in one-inch pots, and then plunged the pots into a moderate heat. A double cover of bell glasses was then placed over them, to exclude the air entirely, which course of treatment was pursued until they had taken root. The shortest time in which this could be accomplished was eight weeks, and the roots were formed in the following manner. First, a callus was formed at the base of the leaf, from which small fibres put forth; a small bud then appeared on the upper side (figure 9); a stalk then arose from this bud, which finally expanded into leaves and formed a perfect plant.

Fig. 9.—LEAF CUTTING.

An English writer remarks, that "the leaves or leaflets of a rose will often take root more freely than even cuttings, and in a much shorter time, but these uniformly refuse to make buds or grow."

This experiment is certainly very curious, and evinces how great, in the vegetable kingdom, are the powers of nature for the maintenance of existence, and is one of those singular results which should lead us to make farther experiments with various parts of plants, and teach us that in Horticulture there is yet a wide field for scientific research.

A favorite mode of propagation with some nurserymen is from soft wood of plants forced in the winter. Many fail entirely in this for want of knowledge of the right condition in which the wood should be before cutting, a condition which cannot be described on paper. Some varieties, like Persian Yellow, will not strike at all, or with great difficulty in this way.

The plants from which these cuttings are to be taken should be prepared and treated as in the preceding chapter. In February and March the cuttings are made and inserted in sand, either in pots or benches, in a house of the same temperature as that in which the parent plant has grown. These pots or benches would be better covered with glass, but it is not essential. After the cuttings have rooted, they can be potted into small pots, and placed in a house of moderate temperature. About the middle of May they can be taken out of these pots and planted in the open ground.

BY LAYERS.

This mode is more particularly applicable to those roses that bloom only once in the year, and which do not strike freely from cuttings, although it can be equally well applied to all the smooth-wooded kinds. It can be performed at midsummer and for several weeks afterward, and should be employed only in those cases where young shoots have been formed at least a foot long and are well matured. The soil should be well dug around the plant, forming a little raised bed of some three feet in diameter, with the soil well pulverized and mixed with some manure thoroughly decomposed, and, if heavy, a little sand. A hole should then be made in this bed about four inches deep, and the young matured shoot bent down into it, keeping the top of the shoot some three or four inches above the surface of the ground; the angle thus being found, which should always be made at a bud and about five or six inches from the top of the shoot, the operator should cut off all the leaves below the ground. A sharp knife should then be placed just below a bud, about three inches below the surface of the ground, and a slanting cut made upward and lengthwise, about half through the branch, forming a sort of tongue from one to two inches long, on the back part of the shoot right opposite the bud; a chip or some of the soil can be placed in the slit, to prevent it from closing, and the shoot can then be carefully laid in the hole, and pegged down at a point some two inches below the cut, keeping, at the same time, the top of the shoot some three or four inches out of the ground, and making it fast to a small stake, to keep it upright. Care should be taken not to make the angle where the branch is pegged at the cut, as the branch would be injured and perhaps broken off; the best place is about two inches below the incision. The soil can then be replaced in the hole, and where it is convenient covered with some moss or litter of any kind. This will protect the soil from the sun and keep it moist, and will materially aid the formation of new roots. These are formed in the same manner as in cuttings; first a callus is produced on those parts of the incision where the bark joins the wood, and from this callus spring the roots, which, in some cases, will have grown sufficiently for the layers to be taken from the parent plant the latter part of the following autumn; in some cases, however, the roots will not have sufficiently formed to allow them to be taken up before another year. The summer is the best period for layering the young shoots. Early in the spring, layers can be made with the wood formed the previous year. Where it is more convenient, a shoot can be rooted by making the incision as above, and introducing it into a quart pot with the bottom partly broken out. This pot can be plunged in the ground, or if the branch is from a standard, it can be raised on a rough platform. In either case, it should be covered with moss, to protect it from the sun, and should be watered every evening. We recollect seeing in the glass manufactories of Paris, a very neat little glass tumbler, used by the French gardeners for this purpose. It held, perhaps, half a pint, and a space about half an inch wide was cut out through the whole length of the side, through which space the branch of any plant was inserted, and the tumbler then filled with soil. When the roots were formed and began to penetrate the soil, they could be easily perceived through the glass. Although an incision is always the most certain, and it is uniformly practiced, roots will in many varieties strike easily from the buds; and a common operation in France is simply to peg down the branches in the soil, without any incision; in some cases, they give the branch a sudden twist, which will break or bruise the bark. and facilitate the formation of roots.

Some Chinese authors state that very long branches may be laid down, and that roots may be thus obtained from all the eyes upon them, which will eventually form as many plants.

Vibert, a well-known rose cultivator in France, remarks upon this point: "Upon laying down with the requisite care some branches fifteen to twenty-four inches long, of the new growth, or of that of the previous year, and upon taking them up with similar care, after twelve or eighteen months, I found only the first eyes expanded into buds or roots, while the rest had perished. I have seldom seen the fifth eye developed, while I have frequently known the whole branch entirely perish. I speak in general terms, for there are some rare exceptions, and the different varieties of the Four-seasons Rose may be cited as proof that a great number of eyes of the same branch have taken root."

This is the opinion of an eminent rose grower; but if, as he states, the Monthly Damask Rose will root freely in this way, many of the smooth-wooded roses would undoubtedly root still more readily, and our rapid growing native rose, Queen of the Prairies, would very probably throw out roots readily, when treated in this manner. It is worth repeated experiment; for, if rapid growing roses, like some of the evergreen varieties, the Greville, and the Queen of the Prairies, could with facility be made to grow in this way, rose hedges could be easily formed by laying down whole branches, and a very beautiful and effective protection would be thus produced, to ornament our fields and gardens.

SUCKERS.

Many roses throw up suckers readily from the root, and often form one of the principal causes of annoyance to the cultivator. For this reason, budding and grafting should always be done on stocks that do not incline to sucker. The Dog Rose—on which almost all the imported varieties are now worked—is particularly liable to this objection, and it is no unusual thing to see half-a-dozen suckers growing about a single rose-tree. When the health and prosperity of the plant are desired, these should be carefully kept down, as they deprive the plant of a material portion of its nourishment. When, however, they are wanted for stocks, they should be taken off every spring with a small portion of root, which can generally be obtained by cutting some distance below the surface of the ground. They should be planted immediately where they are wanted for budding, and will soon be fit for use. Many fine varieties of the summer roses will sucker in this way, and an old plant when taken up will sometimes furnish a large number of thrifty stems, each with a portion of root attached.

BUDDING.

Fifty years ago, budding and grafting were very little practiced, excepting with new varieties, that could with great difficulty be propagated in any other way. Within that time, however, the practice has been constantly increasing until now, when it is extensively employed in Europe, and roses imported from France and England can very rarely be obtained on their own roots. To this mode of propagation, there is one great objection, while the advantages in some varieties are sufficiently great to counterbalance any inconveniences attending the cultivation of a budded or grafted rose. It is generally the case, that the stock or plant on which the Rose is budded is of some variety that will throw up suckers very freely, which growing with great luxuriance, will sometimes overpower the variety budded upon it, and present a mass of its own flowers. The purchaser will thus find a comparatively worthless bloom, instead of the rare and beautiful varieties whose appearance he has been eagerly awaiting, and upon the head of the nurseryman will frequently descend the weight of his indignation. This difficulty can, however, be avoided by a very little attention. The shoot of the stock can very readily be distinguished from that of the budded or grafted variety by its growth and foliage, even if the age of the plant will not allow the point of inoculation to be recognized. In passing the plant in his walks, let the owner simply cut away any shoot of this character that may spring from the stock or root. The budded variety thus receiving all the nourishment from the root, will soon grow with luxuriance, and present to the eager expectant as fine a bloom as he may desire—at the expense only of a little observation, and the trouble of occasionally taking his knife from his pocket.

This trouble, however, is such that the plant is in most cases neglected. Budded or grafted roses are thus very unpopular in this country, and those on their own roots are deemed the only ones which it is safe to plant.

The practice of budding has brought into cultivation a form of the plant which is highly ornamental, but which can never become very general in this country. The Tree Rose is an inoculation upon a standard some four or five feet in height, generally a Dog Rose or Eglantine. The tall, naked stem, a greater part of which is unsheltered by any foliage, is exposed to the full glare of our summer sun, and unless protected in some way, will often die out in two or three years. Its life can be prolonged by covering the stem with moss, or with a sort of tin tube, provided with small holes, to allow the air to enter and circulate around the stem. This is, however, some trouble; and as many will not provide this protection, a large part of the standard roses imported to this country will gradually die out, and rose *bushes* be generally employed for single planting, or for grouping upon the lawn.

In budding, there are two requisites: a well-established and thriftily growing plant, and a well-matured eye or bud. The operation can be performed at any season when these requisites can be obtained. In the open ground, the wood from which the buds are cut is generally not mature until after the first summer bloom.

Having ascertained by running a knife under the bark, that the stock will peel easily, and having some perfectly ripe young shoots with buds upon them, the operation can be performed with a sharp knife that is round and very thin at the point. Make in the bark of the stock a longitudinal incision of three-quarters of an inch, and another short one across the top, as in *a*, fig. 10; run the knife under the bark and loosen it from the wood; then cut from one of the young shoots of the desired variety, a bud, as in *b*; placing the knife a quarter to three-eighths of an

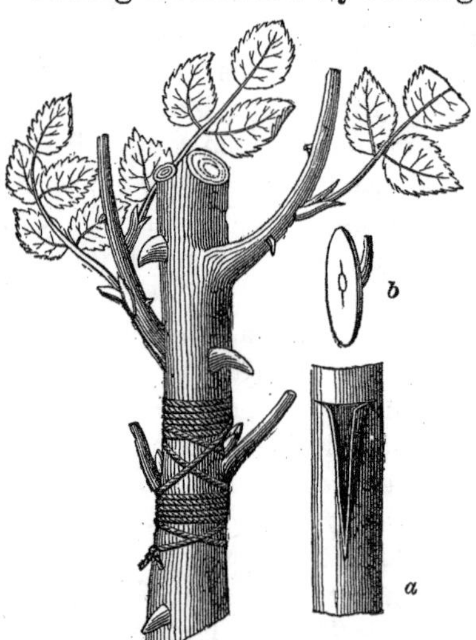

Fig. 10.—BUDDING THE ROSE.

inch above the eye or bud, and cutting out about the same distance below it, cutting sufficiently near the bud to take with it a very thin scale of the wood. English gardeners will always peel off this thin scale; but in our hot climate, it should always be left on, as it assists to keep the bud moist, and does not at all prevent the access of the sap from the stock to the bud. The bud being thus prepared, take it, by the portion of leaf-stalk attached, between the thumb and finger in the left hand, and, with the knife in the right, open the incision in the bark sufficiently to allow the bud to be slipped in as far as it will go, when the bark will close over and retain it. Then take a mat-string, or a piece of yarn, and firmly bind it around the bud, leaving only the petiole and bud exposed, as in *c*, fig. 10. The string should be allowed to remain for about two weeks, or until the bud is united to the stock. If allowed to remain longer, it will sometimes cut into the bark of the rapidly growing stock, but is productive of no other injury. It is the practice with many cultivators to cut off the top of the stock above the bud immediately after inoculation. A limited acquaintance with vegetable physiology would convince the cultivator of the injurious

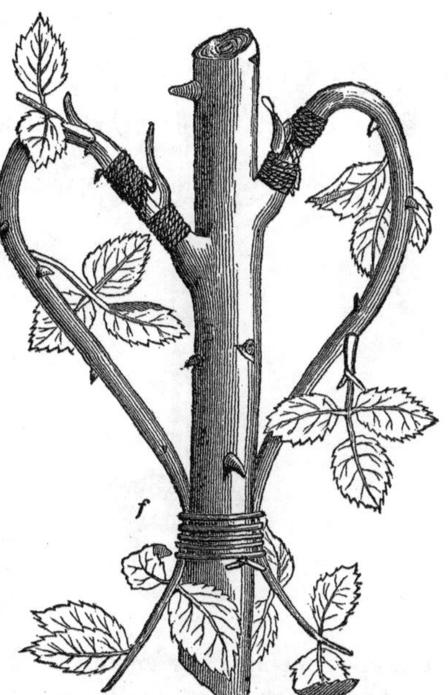

Fig. 11.—BUDDING IN THE BRANCHES.

results of this practice, and that the total excision of the branches of the stock while in full vegetation must be destructive to a large portion of the roots, and highly detrimental to the prosperity of the plant. A much better mode is to bend down the top, and tie its extremity to the lower part of the stock. Several days after this is done, the bud can be inserted just below the sharpest bend of the arch. When the buds are to be placed in the branches of a stock, as in fig. 11, the top of the main stem can be cut off, and the branches arched over and tied to the main stem, as at *f;* the bud is then inserted in each branch, as at *e.* The circulation of the sap being thus impeded by the bending of the branches, it is thrown into the inoculation, and forms then a more immediate union than it would if the branches were not arched. After the buds have become fairly united to the stock and have commenced growing, the top can be safely cut off to the bud, although it would be still better to make the pruning of the top proportionate to the growth of the bud; by this means, a slower, but more healthy vegetation is obtained. When the buds are inserted very late in the season, it is better not to cut off the top of the stock or branches until the following spring, and to preserve the bud dormant. If

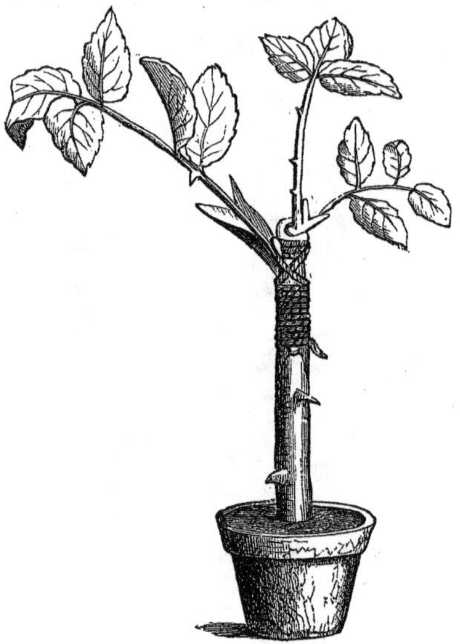

Fig. 12.—BUDDING A POTTED ROSE.

allowed to make a rapid growth so late in the season, there would be great danger of its being killed by frost. European cultivators are very fond of budding several varieties on one stock, in order to obtain the pretty effect produced by a contrast of color. This will only answer where great care is taken to select varieties of the same vegetating force; otherwise one will soon outstrip the others, and appropriate all the nourishment. It is also desirable that they should belong to the same species. When a bud is inserted in a plant in pot, as in fig. 12, the main branches are left, and a portion of the top only cut off, in order to give the bud some additional nourishment.

GRAFTING.

From the pithy nature of the wood of the Rose, grafting is always less certain than budding; but it is frequently adopted by cultivators, as budding cannot be relied upon in the spring, and as there is much wood from the winter pruning which would be otherwise wasted. It is also useful for working over those plants in which buds have missed the previous summer.

There are several modes of grafting, of which the most generally practiced is *cleft-grafting.* For this mode, the stock is cut off at the desired height with a sharp knife, either horizontally, or slightly sloping. The cut should be made just above a bud, which may serve to draw up the sap to the graft. The stock can then be split with a heavy knife, making the slit or cleft about an inch long. The cion should be about four inches long, with two or more buds upon it. An inch of the lower part of the cion can be cut in the shape of a wedge, making one side very thin, and on the thick or outer side, leaving a bud opposite to the top of the wedge. This cion can then be inserted in the cleft as far as the wedge is cut, being very careful to make the bark of the cion fit exactly to that of the stock. In order to exclude the air, the top and side of the stock should then be bound with a strip of cloth covered with a composition of beeswax and resin in equal parts, with sufficient tallow to make it soft at a reasonably low temperature. In the course of two or three weeks,

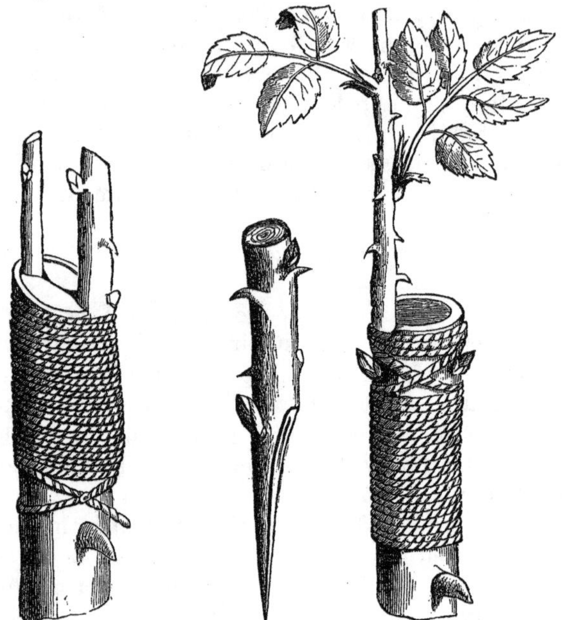

Fig. 13.—CLEFT GRAFTING. Fig. 14.—WHIP GRAFTING.

if every thing is favorable, the cion will begin to unite, and will be ready to go forward with advancing vegetation. When the stock is sufficiently large, two cions can be inserted, as in fig. 13.

Whip-grafting is performed by cutting a slice of bark with a little wood from the side of a stock about an inch and a half long, and then paring a cion of the usual length down to a very thin lower extremity, as in fig. 14. This cion can then be accurately fitted on to the place from which the slice of bark and wood is taken. The whole can then be bound around with cotton cloth, covered with the composition described before. In all grafting it should be borne in mind, that it is essential for the bark of the cion and that of the stock to touch each other in some point, and the more the points of contact, the greater will be the chance of success.

Rind-grafting is also sometimes practiced, but is more uncertain than the former, as the swelling of the stock is very apt to force the cion out. This mode must be practiced when the bark peels easily, or separates with ease from the wood. The top of the stock must be cut off square, and the bark cut through from the top about an inch downward. The point of the knife can then be inserted at the top, and the bark peeled back, as in *a*, fig. 15. It is desirable, as before, that a bud should be left on the other side of the stock, opposite this opening; and the French prefer, also, to have a bud left on the outside of the part of the cion which is inserted. The cion should be cut out and sloped flat on one side, as in *b*, fig. 15; then inserted in the stock between the bark and wood, as in *c*, and bound with mat-strings, or strips of grafting cloth.

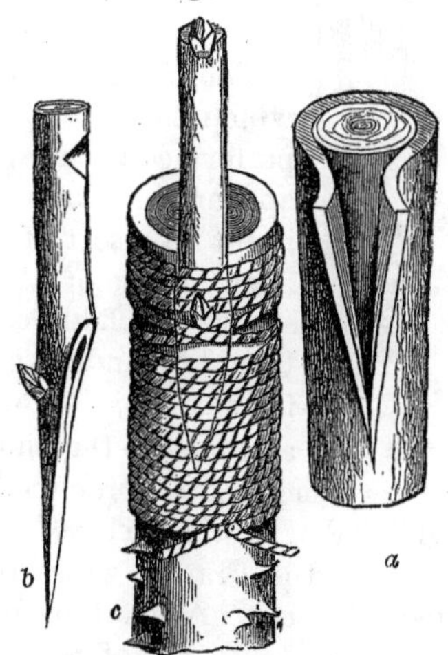

Fig. 15.—RIND GRAFTING.

The French have another mode of grafting stocks about the size of a quill or the little finger. It is done by placing the knife about two inches below a bud which is just on the point of starting, and cutting half way through the stock, and two inches down, as in fig. 16. The cion is then placed in the lower part of this cavity, in the same manner as with cleft grafting. This mode is called *Aspirant*, from the bud above the incision, which continues to draw up the sap, until the development of the cion. When the cion has grown about two inches, the top of the stock is cut off and covered with grafting wax. This mode is not always successful, as the sap sometimes leaves the side of the stock which has been partly cut away and passes up the other side.

Fig. 16.

The French have also a mode of grafting, which they call *par incrustation*, and which is performed in the spring, as soon as the leaf-buds appear. A cion with a bud adhering to the wood is cut in a sort of oval shape, and inserted in a cavity made of the same shape, and just below an eye which has commenced growing. It is then bound around with matting, as in budding. This is a sort of spring budding, with rather more wood attached to the bud, than in summer budding. It is very successfully practiced by various cultivators in the vicinity of Paris. There is still another mode sometimes practiced in France, which owes its origin to a cultivator named Lecoq. A small branch is chosen, which is provided with two buds, one of them being on the upper part, and the other near its larger end. A sidelong sloping cut is made all along its lower half, the upper being left entire. When the cion is thus prepared, its cut side is fitted to the side of the stock under the bark, which has been cut and peeled back. It is then bound around with mat-strings or grafting cloth in the usual way. This mode has a peculiar merit; should the upper bud not grow, the lower one rarely fails, and develops itself as in common budding.

Cleft and whip-grafting is also practiced occasionally upon the roots of the Rose, and succeeds very well with some varieties. These modes of grafting can all be more successfully practiced on stocks in pots in green-houses with bottom heat and bell glasses. We have given thus concisely, and, we hope, clearly, the various modes of budding and grafting with which we are acquainted. They may be sufficient to enable the amateur to amuse his leisure hours, though his success may not entirely meet his expectations. Simple as these operations are, they require a kind of skill, and, if we may so call it, sleight-of-hand, which is only attained by constant practice upon a great number of plants.

CHAPTER VIII.

MULTIPLICATION BY SEED AND HYBRIDIZING.

We have described, in former pages, the various modes of cultivating the Rose, and of propagating the many beautiful varieties which exist, and would now briefly advert to a mode of developing still farther the beauty which lies hid within the horny covering that protects the dormant germ of vitality—in other words, of obtaining new varieties by seed. With the making of the seed-bed commenced a new era in the culture of the Rose, and advancing with rapid strides, it made more progress in forty years than in centuries before. The Dutch seem to have been the first to raise roses from seed, by the same mode which they applied successfully to their tulips, hyacinths, etc., and from the time that this mode became generally employed, the varieties of roses began to increase. In this species of cultivation the French soon outstripped their Dutch neighbors, and gained the reputation which they still retain, of preëminent skill in the production of new varieties of roses from the seed.

From 1805 to 1810, the Empress Josephine, whose love for flowers is well known, collected at her favorite residence, Malmaison, the choicest varieties of the Rose that could be obtained from Holland, Germany, and Belgium, and thus gave an increased impulse to the culture of roses in the vicinity of Paris.

According to De Pronville, a French writer, there were, in 1814, only 182 varieties of roses, and the advantage of multiplication by seed is sufficiently evinced by the fact that there are now more than 6,000 varieties, the poorest of which are much better than any which existed at that day. Among the earliest cultivators of roses from the seed, were three Frenchmen: Dupont, Vilmorin, and Descemet. The former was the gardener of the Empress Josephine. When the allied armies entered Paris, in 1815, the garden of Descemet contained 10,000 seedling roses, which Vibert, in his anxiety to secure from destruction, succeeded in carrying to his garden in the interior.

In England, very little attention seems, at that time, to have been paid to the production of new varieties from seed, and the English relied very much upon the continent for their choice roses. Now, however, they are abundantly redeeming their reputation, and many fine varieties have been produced by English rose-growers, at the head of whom stands Rivers, whose efforts are seconded by Wood, Paul, Lane, and others. They are still, however, compelled to yield to the French cultivators; for to these we are indebted for our very finest roses—for Lamarque, Solfaterre, La Reine, Chromatella, the new white Perpetuals, Souvenir de Malmaison, and others.

The varieties of roses became increasingly great after the introduction of the Bengals, Noisettes, Teas, and Bourbons—all these classes producing readily from seed, and in endless variety. There still remains a willingness to cast aside the old for the new, and however much we may regret this disposition, for the sake of some old and truly deserving favorites, we cannot feel willing to denounce it, for it exhibits a gratifying evidence of a desire for improvement, and the existence of a spirit of progress, which, dissatisfied with things as they are, is continually striving after nearer approaches to perfection. If, in this strife, some of our old favorites have been cast aside, we are more than abundantly compensated for their loss by the new claimants to our regard.

Those who intend to raise new roses from seed should select varieties differing as much as possible in color and habit, and possessing broad, thick, and well-formed petals; their stamens should also be visible, and their pistils perfect; for perfectly double flowers, in which all the organs of propagation—the stamens and pistils—are changed into petals, never yield seed. These should be planted together in a rich soil, and as far as possible from any other roses. If there are among them any two varieties whose peculiarities it is desired to unite in a single plant, place these next to each other, and there may possibly be such an admixture of the pollen as will produce the desired result.

Care should be taken not to affect the proper maturity of the seed by taking off the petals, but allow them to fall by their own decay. The seed should be perfectly mature before it is gathered, which will be immediately after the first hard frost. After the hips have been gathered, the seeds can be taken out with the point of a knife, or, if there is a large quantity, they can be put on a table and bruised with a wooden roller; the covering of the seeds is so tough that they cannot easily be injured. When the hip is sufficiently bruised, it can be plunged into a vessel of water; and by continued friction, the seeds can be easily separated from the pulp which surrounds them, and will generally fall to the bottom. After being dried a few days in the shade, they should be placed just beneath the surface, in pots filled with fine sand, or peat earth, where they can be kept until wanted for planting in the spring. The seeds which are not thus placed in sand soon after they are gathered will not grow until the second, and if delayed very long, until the third year. In this case, however, their germination can be hastened by sowing them in earthen pans, which are placed upon a hot-bed or under a glass frame. The seeds being thus planted immediately after being gathered, the sand should be kept moistened through the winter, and the pots put out of the reach of frost. Mice are very fond of these seeds, and will destroy them unless they are protected. The pots should be kept out of all heat, excepting what may be required to keep the frost from them, until the first of April, in this latitude, and at the South, earlier; this is requisite, in order to prevent their germinating before all danger of frost is past in the open air. At the time the pots or pans are brought from their sheltered place into a warm temperature, beds for the plants should be made in the open air, that they may be ready the moment they are required. For these an eastern aspect is the best, and in our hot climate, on the north side of a fence would answer very well; if they are in an open piece of ground, they should be sheltered by an awning from the hot sun. The soil should be a rich, light sandy mould, with a little peat, if convenient, and should be finely pulverized. The seeds should now be closely watched, and the moment they are seen pushing up the sand, in order to obtain light, they should be taken out singly with the point of a knife, taking a small portion of the sand with them. The bed having been previously watered, and raked fine, drills can be made, half an inch deep and about a foot apart, in which the germinating seeds can be placed, at a distance of six inches from each other, and then carefully covered with finely pulverized soil. Having commenced germinating in the pots, the seeds, now in the genial warmth of a spring sun, but protected from its fiercest rays, will soon show their heads above the ground, and striking deep root in the rich soil, grow rapidly. While the plants are small, care should be taken to keep the ground constantly moist.

We are aware that this process is somewhat new with rose seeds, although it has been long practiced with Rhododendrons and other plants, but we are convinced of its superiority to the old mode. The delicate roots of young plants are very susceptible of injury by change, and many are frequently lost by the first potting; this risk is avoided by transplanting the seed before the first root fibre is formed, and when, being in the act of germination, there can be no possible danger of its rotting, which is frequently a serious objection to sowing seeds at once in the open ground. The trouble and risk of loss occasioned by subsequent re-pottings are also avoided, and the plants have, by this mode, full liberty to grow as luxuriantly as they choose, with only the slight attention required by watering and shading. As the plan of Rivers is materially different, we will give his directions in detail, admitting, at the same time, that, under some circumstances, it may be preferable to that we have presented above.

"The hips of all the varieties of roses, will, in general, be fully ripe by the beginning of November; they should then be gathered and kept entire, in a flower pot filled with dry sand, carefully guarded from mice. In February, or by the first week in March, they must be broken to pieces with the fingers, and sown in flower pots, such as are generally used for sowing seeds in, called 'seed pans'; but for rose seeds they should not be too shallow; nine inches in depth will be enough. These should be nearly, but not quite, filled with a rich compost of rotten manure and sandy loam, or peat; the seeds may be covered, to the depth of about half an inch, with the same compost; a piece of kiln wire must then be placed over the pot, fitting closely at the rim, so as to prevent the ingress of mice, which are passionately fond of rose seeds; there must be space enough between the wire and the mould for the young plants to come up—half an inch will probably be found enough; the pots of seed must never be placed under glass, but kept constantly in the open air, in a full sunny exposure, as the wire will shade the mould and prevent its drying. Water should be given occasionally, in dry weather. The young plants will perhaps make their appearance in April or May, but very often the seed does not vegetate until the second spring. When they have made their 'rough leaves,' that is, when they have three or four leaves, they must be carefully raised with the point of a narrow pruning-knife, potted into small pots, and placed in the shade; if the weather is very hot and dry, they may be covered with a handglass for a few days. They may remain in those pots a month, and then be planted out into a rich border; by the end of August those that are robust growers will have made shoots long enough for budding." Until the plants have become firmly rooted, and, in fact, through the most of the first summer, they should be protected from the heat of the sun; a cheap mode of doing this is to put up rough posts, connect them by pieces of wood, lay rough slats across these, and cover the whole with straw or cornstalks; but a much neater covering is a good canvas awning, supported by posts, which can be taken down when not needed, and will last many years. The Bourbons and Bengals, with the Teas and Noisettes, will sometimes bloom the first season; but as the plant will be weak, a correct opinion cannot be formed of its character until the second summer. The summer roses, or those which bloom only once in the season, never show bloom until their third, and sometimes not until their fourth and fifth year. It is well to let all the plants remain in the seed-bed until the fifth year, as some which prove unpromising at first may result in something really good. All that prove bad the fifth year can be marked for destruction, or cut down to receive the buds of the good varieties. In order to obtain a good bloom as soon as possible, it is well to have ready some strong stocks of the Greville, Mannetti, or any other free-growing rose, into which buds can be inserted of any of the seedlings whose habit and general appearance promise good flowers, and whose growth has been sufficient to furnish good buds. The next spring the stock should be cut down to the bud, which will then make luxuriant shoots, and produce flowers the same season, if an Everblooming variety; but if one of the Summer roses, not until the next season. The third spring let every branch be cut down to three or four eyes, when it will more fully develop its character, and will often continue improving until its fifth or sixth year.

The first winter, the young plants will require protection from the cold by some kind of litter, and the Bengal, Tea, and Noisette varieties will always need it during the winter. Where there are any plants of these latter, whose habit and appearance promise something excellent, they can be potted on the approach of winter, kept in a cool temperature, free from frost, and replanted in the spring.

When it is desired that the young plant should possess the properties of two well-known flowers, resort is had to artificial impregnation.

Although the existence of sexuality in plants appears to have been known to the ancients, and is mentioned not only by Pliny, Claudian, and Theophrastus, but also by Ebu-Alwan, in a work on agriculture written originally in Chaldaic; yet it does not seem to have been generally admitted by botanists, until announced by Linnæus in 1731. From this time the possibility of the existence of hybrid plants was admitted, and Linnæus, with many subsequent authors, published observations tending to show that, even in the natural state, new species were formed by two different plants, the pistil of one having been fecundated by the stamens of the other. This impregnation has been artificially applied, by modern cultivators, to the production of new varieties of fruits and flowers. With the Geranium, Fuchsia, Pæony, Pansy, and other flowers, it has produced remarkable results. The mode of impregnating the Rose artificially has been so little practiced with us, and has been so well described by Rivers, that we prefer detailing the process in his own words:

"When it is desirable the qualities of a favorite rose should preponderate, the petals of the flower to be fertilized must be opened gently with the fingers. A flower that will expand in the morning should be opened the afternoon or evening previous, and the anthers all removed with a pair of pointed scissors. The following morning, when this flower is fully expanded, it must be fertilized with a flower of some variety of whose qualities it is desired to have seedlings largely partake. It requires some watchfulness to open the petals at the proper time; if too soon, the petals will be injured in forcing them open, and in hot weather, in July, if delayed only an hour or two, the anthers will be found to have shed their pollen. To ascertain precisely when the pollen is in a fit state for transmission, a few of the anthers should be gently pressed with the finger and thumb; if the yellow dust adheres to them, the operation may be performed; it requires close examination and some practice to know when the flower to be operated upon is in a fit state to receive the pollen; as a general rule, the flowers ought to be in the same state of expansion, or, in other words, about the same age.

"To exemplify the process, we will suppose that a climbing Moss Rose, with red or crimson flowers, is wished for: the flowers of the Blush Ayrshire, which bear seed abundantly, may be selected, and before expansion, the anthers removed; the following morning, or as soon after the operation as these flowers open, they should be fertilized with those of the Luxembourg Moss; if the operation succeed, seed will be procured, from which, the probability is, that a climbing rose will be produced with the habit and flowers of the Moss Rose, or at least an approximation to them. I mention the union of the Moss and Ayrshire Roses by way of illustration, and merely to point out to the amateur how extensive and how interesting a field of operations is open in this way. I ought to give a fact that has occurred in my own experience, which will tell better with the sceptical than a thousand anticipations. About four years since, in a pan of seedling Moss Roses, was one with a most peculiar habit, even when very young; this has since proved a hybrid rose, partaking much more of the Scotch Rose than of any other, and until the plant arrived at full growth, I thought it a Scotch Rose, the seed of which had by accident been mixed with that of the Moss Rose, although I had taken extreme care. To my surprise it has since proved a perfect hybrid, having the sepals and the fruit of the Provence Rose, with the spiny and dwarf habit of the Scotch Rose; it bears abundance of hips, which are all abortive. The difference in the fruit of the Moss and Provence Rose, and that of the Scotch, is very remarkable; and this it was which drew my particular attention to the plant in question. It was raised from the same seed, and in the same seed-pan, as the single crimson Moss Rose. As this strange hybrid came from a Moss Rose accidentally fertilized, we may expect that art will do much more for us.

"It is only in cases where it is wished for the qualities of a particular rose to predominate, that the removal of the anthers of the rose to be fertilized is necessary: thus, if a yellow climbing rose is desired by the union of the Yellow Brier with the Ayrshire, every anther should be removed from the latter, so that it is fertilized solely with the pollen of the former. In some cases, where it is desirable to have the qualities of both parents in an equal degree, the removal of the anthers must not take place: thus I have found, by removing them from the Luxembourg Moss, and fertilizing that rose with a dark variety of *Rosa Gallica*, that the features of the Moss Rose are totally lost in its offspring, and they become nearly pure varieties of the former; but if the anthers of the Moss Rose are left untouched, and it is fertilized with *Rosa Gallica*, interesting hybrids are the result, more or less mossy."

There is no branch of rose culture possessing more interest for the amateur, with whose leisure its prosecution is compatible. The constant care and attention required, in order to ensure success, place it in a great measure beyond the limits of a large commercial establishment. The great desideratum at this time is a double, yellow, climbing rose. If the Harrison Rose were fertilized with the Queen of the Prairies, or the latter with the Solfaterre or Chromatella, a rose might possibly be obtained with the rich yellow of the Harrison Rose, and the robust habit and beautifully formed flower of the Queen of the Prairies. While, however, we recommend this mode of artificial impregnation, we would by no means discourage the sowing of seeds whose flowers have not thus been fecundated. The seed of the Harrison Rose, or of any of the yellow roses, may, if perseveringly saved from generation to generation, produce a yellow climbing rose. In fact, we are inclined to think that among all the reputed hybrids, a much less number than is supposed owe their origin to a crossed fecundation. It is a fact generally admitted by botanists, that all varieties of plants will generally produce from their seed plants very dissimilar, preserving, perhaps, some peculiarities of their parents, but differing in many essential particulars.

It will thus be perceived that, in the simple sowing of seeds, where there is a dislike to the trouble of artificial impregnation, there is a wide field for experiment and for successful result. But to those who have the leisure and the patience to transfer from one plant to another its fertilizing matter, it forms a pleasant amusement, with rather a greater probability of satisfactory results. In either case, every amateur of roses should have his seed-plat; and if, out of a thousand, or even five thousand roses, he should obtain one good variety, and differing from any other known, he will be conferring an important service upon rose-culture, and will encourage others to pursue the same course, until we shall be in no wise behind either France or England in this interesting branch of horticulture.

CHAPTER IX.

DISEASES AND INSECTS ATTACKING THE ROSE.

Brave Rose, alas, whose art thou? In thy chair
  Where thou didst lately so triumph and shine
A worm doth sit, whose many feet and hair
  Are the more foul the more thou art divine.
This, this hath done it; this did bite the root
  And bottom of the leaves, which, when the wind
Did once perceive, it blew them under foot,
  Where rude, unhallow'd steps do crush and grind
    Their beauteous glories. Only shreds of thee,
    And those all bitten, in thy chair I see.

HERBERT.

The diseases to which the Rose is liable are generally owing either to the presence of various Cryptogamic plants, or to the attacks of certain insects whose larvæ are supported at the expense of the plant. Among Cryptogamic parasites which have been observed upon rose-bushes, and which infest chiefly the Provence and other rough-leaved roses, the following are the most troublesome:

Rust.—The rust, when examined by a magnifier, is found to consist of minute yellow spots, each of which is a fungus, *Lecythea Rosæ.* It is common and injurious to roses, as it frequently covers all the leaves. The most effectual mode of preventing its spreading is to cut off with care and burn all the infected branches, which will sometimes render necessary the destruction of the whole plant.

Mildew.—The minute fungus which produces mildew is called by botanists *Sphærotheca pannosa.* It appears like a gray mould on the smaller stems and blistered leaves. It is a very troublesome enemy to the Rose, and will sometimes put at defiance every application for its destruction. The most effectual is smoking with sulphur, dusting with dry flowers of sulphur, or syringing with sulphur water. The former should only be practiced by a skillful hand, as too much sulphur-smoke will sometimes entirely kill the plant.

Mould is due to a minute gray fungus, *Peronospora sparsa*, and manifests its presence by the appearance of irregular pale brownish spots upon the upper surface of the leaf. Upon the under surface of these spots the mould will be found.

Other species of fungi attack the Rose, but they are not sufficiently troublesome to the cultivator to need enumeration here.

The *insects* which infest the Rose are quite numerous, and their attacks are more or less injurious. The majority of those which are found on the plant in the state of perfect insects are comparatively harmless. The most injurious are those whose larvæ feed on the leaves and pith of the trunk and limbs, and thus destroy the plant; while the perfect insect, like the Green-fly, will simply stop the growth and impair the health of the tree, by fastening upon the green and tender bark of the young shoots, and devouring the sap. It is highly desirable that amateur cultivators should devote more time to the study of Entomology, for upon an intimate acquaintance with the habits of these minute depredators depends, in a greater degree than is generally supposed, the success of cultivation. Our own leisure is so limited, that we have been able to devote very little time to this subject; and we can find no work that treats in detail the insects that attack the Rose. We simply give some account of the most troublesome ones drawn mainly from Harris' Insects Injurious to Vegetation.

Green-Fly, or **Plant-Louse.**—*Aphis Rosæ.*—This very common insect is a scourge to roses, from the facility of its reproduction, and its numerous progeny sometimes entirely cover the leaves, the young sprouts, and the flower buds. Devouring the sap, they are very injurious, and, when numerous, sometimes destroy the plant, while they soil every part on which they collect. The most common species is of a pale green, but there is a variety of a dingy yellow. Many are destroyed by small birds, but they have other enemies, as the larvæ of the *Coccinellas*, or Lady-birds, and other insects destroy large numbers. The first eggs of the Green-fly are deposited in the autumn, at the base of the buds, and are hatched in the early part of the following spring. Generation after generation is then rapidly produced, numbering sometimes eight or ten before autumn. These are produced alive, and without the intervention of the male. Reaumur estimated that a single Aphis might produce six thousand millions in one summer. The first hatching can be prevented by washing the plant with soft soap and water, or with whale-oil soap, before the buds commence swelling. When the plant is infested with them, it can be washed with tobacco-water and then rinsed in clean water. If in a house, fumigation with tobacco is better. An English writer recommends washing in a decoction of an ounce of quassia to a quart of water, as a very effective and safe remedy. Fumigation is, however, the most thoroughly searching remedy, and can be easily applied to plants in the open air, by means of an empty barrel inverted over the plant, and a pan of burning tobacco.

Gall-Flies.—Several species of *Cynips*, or Gall-flies, attack the rose, their punctures, made for the purpose of depositing their eggs, being followed by variously formed excrescences containing the larvæ. The Bedequars, formed by the puncture of the *Cynips Rosæ*, were formerly employed in medicine as astringents. Harris enumerates the American species as follows:

Cynips bicolor.—"Round, prickly galls, of a reddish

color, and rather larger than a pea, may often be seen on rose-bushes. Each of them contains a single grub, and this in due time turns to a gall-fly. Its head and thorax are black, and rough with numerous little pits; its hind-body is polished, and, with the legs, of a brownish-red color. It is a large insect compared with the size of its gall, measuring nearly one-fifth of an inch in length, while the diameter of its gall, not including the prickles, rarely exceeds three-tenths of an inch."

Cynips dichlocerus, "or the gall-fly with two-colored antennæ, is of a brownish-red or cinnamon color, with four little longitudinal grooves on the top of the thorax, the lower part of the antennæ red, and the remainder black. It varies in being darker sometimes, and measures from one-eighth to three-sixteenths of an inch in length. Great numbers of these gall-flies are bred in the irregular woody galls, or long excrescences, of the stems of rose-bushes."

Cynips semipiceus.—"The small roots of rose-bushes, and of other plants of the same family, sometimes produce rounded, warty, and woody knobs, inhabited by numerous gall-insects, which, in coming out, pierce them with small holes on all sides. The winged insects closely resemble the dark varieties of the preceding species in color, and in the little furrows on the thorax; but their legs are rather paler, and they do not measure more than one-tenth of an inch in length."

Rose-Slug, *Selandria Rosæ*, of Harris, who gives the following account: "The saw-fly of the rose, which, as it does not seem to have been described before, may be called *Selandria Rosæ*, from its favorite plant, so nearly resembles the slug-worm saw-fly as not to be distinguished therefrom except by a practiced observer. It is also very much like *Selandria barda*, *Vitis*, and *pygmæa*, but has not the red thorax of these three closely allied species. It is of a deep and shining black color. The first two pairs of legs are brownish-gray or dirty white, except the thighs, which are almost entirely black. The hind legs are black, with whitish knees. The wings are smoky, and transparent, with dark brown veins, and a brown spot near the middle of the edge of the first pair. The body of the male is a little more than three-twentieths of an inch long, that of the female one-fifth of an inch or more, and the wings expand nearly or quite two-fifths of an inch. These saw-flies come out of the ground at various times between the twentieth of May and the middle of June, during which period they pair and lay their eggs. The females do not fly much, and may be seen, during most of the day, resting on the leaves; and, when touched, they draw up their legs, and fall to the ground. The males are more active, fly from one rose-bush to another, and hover around their sluggish partners. The latter, when about to lay their eggs, turn a little on one side, unsheathe their saws, and thrust them obliquely into the skin of the leaf, depositing in each incision thus made, a single egg. The young begin to hatch in ten days or a fortnight after the eggs are laid. They may sometimes be found on the leaves as early as the first of June, but do not usually appear in considerable numbers until the twentieth of the same month. How long they are in coming to maturity, I have not particularly observed; but the period of their existence in the caterpillar state probably does not exceed three weeks. They somewhat resemble the young of the saw-fly in form, but are not quite so convex. They have a small, round, yellowish head, with a black dot on each side of it, and are provided with twenty-two short legs. The body is green above, paler at the sides, and yellowish beneath; and it is soft, and almost transparent like jelly. The skin of the back is transversely wrinkled, and covered with minute elevated points; and there are two small, triple-pointed warts on the edge of the first ring, immediately behind the head. These gelatinous and sluggish creatures eat the upper surface of the leaf in large irregular patches, leaving the veins and the skin beneath untouched; and they are sometimes so thick that not a leaf on the bushes is spared by them, and the whole foliage looks as if it had been scorched by fire, and drops off soon afterward. They cast their skins several times, leaving them extended and fastened on the leaves; after the last moulting they lose their semi-transparent and greenish color, and acquire an opaque yellowish hue. They then leave the rose-bushes, some of them slowly creeping down the stem, and others rolling up and dropping off, especially when the bushes are shaken by the wind. Having reached the ground, they burrow to the depth of an inch or more in the earth, where each one makes for itself a small oval cell, of grains of earth, cemented with a little gummy silk. Having finished their transformations, and turned to flies, within their cells, they come out of the ground early in August, and lay their eggs for a second brood of young. These, in turn, perform their appointed work of destruction in the autumn; they then go into the ground, make their earthy cells, remain therein throughout the winter, and appear in the winged form, in the following spring and summer.

"During several years past, these pernicious vermin have infested the rose-bushes in the vicinity of Boston, and have proved so injurious to them, as to have excited the attention of the Massachusetts Horticultural Society, by whom a premium of one hundred dollars for the most successful mode of destroying these insects was offered in the summer of 1840. About ten years ago, I observed them in gardens in Cambridge, and then made myself acqainted with their transformations. At that time they had not reached Milton, my former place of residence, and have appeared in that place only within two or three years. They now seem to be gradually extending in all directions, and an effectual method for preserving our roses from their attacks has become very desirable to all persons who set any value on this beautiful ornament of our gardens and shrubberies. Showering or syringing the bushes with a liquor, made by mixing with water the juice expressed from tobacco by tobacconists, has been recommended; but some caution is necessary in making this mixture of a proper strength, for if too strong, it is injurious to plants; and the experiment does not seem, as yet, to have been conducted with sufficient care to insure safety and success. Dusting lime over the plants when wet with dew has been tried, and found of some use; but this and all other remedies will probably yield in efficacy to Mr. Haggerston's mixture of whale-oil soap and water, in the proportion of two pounds of the soap to fifteen gallons of water. Particular directions, drawn up by Mr. Haggerston himself, for the preparation and use of this simple and cheap application, may be found in the "Boston Courier" for the 25th of June, 1841, and also in most of our agricultural and horticultural journals of the same time. The utility of this mixture has already been repeatedly mentioned in this treatise, and it may be applied in other cases with advantage. Mr. Haggerston finds that it effectually destroys many kinds of insects; and he particularly mentions plant-lice of various kinds, red spiders, canker-worms, and a little jumping insect which has lately been found quite as hurtful to rose-bushes as the slugs or young of the saw-fly."

Rose-Bug.—*Macrodactylus subspinosa.*—"Common as this insect is in the vicinity of Boston, it is, or was a few years ago, unknown in the northern and western parts of Massachusetts, in New Hampshire, and in Maine. It may, therefore, be well to give a brief description of it. This beetle measures seven-twentieths of an inch in length. Its body is slender, tapers before and behind, and is entirely covered with very short and close ashen-yellow down; the thorax is long and narrow, angularly widened in the middle of each side, which suggested the name *subspinosa*, or somewhat spined; the legs are slender, and of a pale red color; the joints of the feet are tipped with black, and are very long, which caused Latreille to call the genus *Macrodactylus*, that is, long toe, or long foot. The natural history of the rose-chafer, one of the greatest scourges with which our gardens and nurseries have been afflicted, was for a long time involved in mystery, but is at last fully cleared up. The prevalence of this insect on the rose, and its annual appearance, coinciding with the blossoming of that flower, have gained for it the popular name by which it is here known. For some time after they were first noticed, rose-bugs appeared to be confined to their favorite, the blossoms of the rose; but within thirty years, they have prodigiously increased in number, have attacked at random various kinds of plants in swarms, and have become notorious for their extensive and deplorable ravages. The grape-vine in particular, the cherry, plum, and apple-trees, have annually suffered by their depredations; many other fruit-trees and shrubs, garden vegetables and corn, and even the trees of the forest, and the grass of the fields, have been laid under contribution by these indiscriminate feeders, by whom leaves, flowers, and fruits are alike consumed. The unexpected arrival of these insects in swarms, at their first coming, and their sudden disappearance at the close of their career, are remarkable facts in their history. They come forth from the ground during the second week in June, or about the time of the blossoming of the Damask Rose, and remain from thirty to forty days. At the end of this period the males become exhausted, fall to the ground, and perish, while the females enter the earth, lay their eggs, return to the surface, and, after lingering a few days, die also. The eggs laid by each female are about thirty in number, and are deposited from one to four inches beneath the surface of the soil; they are nearly globular, whitish, and about one-thirtieth of an inch in diameter, and are hatched twenty days after they are laid. The young larvæ begin to feed on such tender roots as are within their reach. Like other grubs of the Scarabæians, when not eating, they lie upon the side, with the body curved, so that the head and tail are nearly in contact; they move with difficulty on a level surface, and are continually falling over on one side or the other.

"They attain their full size in autumn, being then nearly three-quarters of an inch long, and about an eighth of an inch in diameter. They are of a yellowish white color, with a tinge of blue towards the hinder extremity, which is thick and obtuse, or rounded; a few short hairs are scattered on the surface of the body; there are six short legs, namely, a pair to each of the first three rings behind the head, and the latter is covered with a horny shell of a pale rust color. In October they descend below the reach of frost, and pass the winter in a torpid state. In the spring they approach toward the surface, and each one forms for itself a little cell, of an oval shape, by turning round a great many times, so as to compress the earth, and render the inside of the cavity hard and smooth. Within this cell the grub is transformed to a pupa, during the month of May, by casting off its skin, which is pushed downward in folds from the head to the tail. The pupa has somewhat the form of the perfected beetle, but it is of a yellowish white color, and its short, stump-like wings, its antennæ, and its legs, are folded upon the breast, and its whole body is inclosed in a thin film that wraps each part separately. During the month of June this filmy skin is rent, the included beetle withdraws from its body and its limbs, bursts open its earthen cell, and digs its way to the surface of the ground. Thus the various changes from the egg to the full development of the perfected beetle are completed within the space of one year.

"Such being the metamorphoses and habits of these insects, it is evident that we cannot attack them in the egg, the grub, or the pupa state; the enemy, in these stages, is beyond our reach, and is subject to the control only of the natural but unknown means appointed by the Author of Nature to keep the insect tribes in check. When they have issued from their subterranean retreats, and have congregated upon our vines, trees, and other vegetable productions in the complete enjoyment of their propensities, we must unite our efforts to seize and crush the invaders. They must indeed be crushed, scalded, or burned, to deprive them of life, for they are not affected by any of the applications usually found destructive to other insects. Experience has proved the utility of gathering them by hand, or of shaking them, or brushing them from the plants into tin vessels containing a little water. They should be collected daily during the period of their visitation, and should be committed to the flames, or killed by scalding water. The late John Lowell, Esq., states, that in 1823, he discovered on a solitary apple-tree the rose-bugs 'in vast numbers, such as could not be described, and would not be believed if they were described, or at least none but an ocular witness could conceive of their numbers. Destruction by hand was out of the question' in this case. He put sheets under the tree, and shook them down and burned them. Dr. Green, of Mansfield, whose investigations have thrown much light on the history of this insect, proposes protecting plants with millinet, and says that in this way only did he succeed in securing his grape-vines from depredation. His remarks also show the utility of gathering them. 'Eighty-six of these spoilers,' says he, 'were known to infest a single rose-bud, and were crushed with one grasp of the hand.' Suppose, as was probably the case, that one-half of them were females; by this destruction, eight hundred eggs, at least, were prevented from becoming matured.

During the time of their prevalence, rose-bugs are sometimes found in immense numbers on the flowers of the common white-weed, or ox-eye daisy, (*Chrysanthemum leucanthemum*,) a worthless plant, which has come to us from Europe, and has been suffered to overrun our pastures, and encroach on our mowing lands. In certain cases it may become expedient rapidly to mow down the infested white-weed in dry pastures, and consume it with the sluggish rose-bugs on the spot.

"Our insect-eating birds undoubtedly devour many of these insects, and deserve to be cherished and protected for their services. Rose-bugs are also eaten greedily by domesticated fowls; and when they become exhausted and fall to the ground, or when they are about to lay their eggs, they are destroyed by moles, insects, and other animals, which lie in wait to seize them. Dr. Green informs us that a species of dragon-fly, or devil's needle, devours them. He also says that an insect, which he calls the enemy of the cut-worm, probably the larva of a Carabus, or predaceous ground-beetle, preys on the grubs of the common dor-bug. In France, the golden ground-beetle (*Carabus auratus*) devours the female dor or chafer at the moment when she is about to deposit her eggs. I have taken one specimen of this fine ground-beetle in Massachusetts, and we have several other kinds equally predaceous, which probably contribute to check the increase of our native Melolonthians."—*Harris.*

A. J. Downing recommends the use of open-mouthed bottles, half filled (and occasionally renewed) with a mixture of sweetened water and vinegar, and placed about the plant. He also recommends pouring boiling water on the ground, under the bushes, at the first appearance of the insects, and before their wings are formed. They nearly all rise to the surface of the ground, and emerge about the same time that the Damask Rose first begins to open. A little observation will enable the cultivator to seize the right time for the scalding operation.

Rose Leaf-Hopper.—*Tettigonia Rosæ* of Harris, who states that it has been mistaken for the Vine-fretter, or Thrips. It is yellowish white, and about three-twentieths of an inch long; the male has two recurved appendages at the tip of its hind body. Dr. Harris says, "Swarms of these insects may be found in various stages of growth on the leaves of the rose-bush through the greater part of summer, and even in winter upon housed plants. Their numerous cast skins may be seen adhering to the lower side of the leaves. They pair and lay their eggs about the middle of June, and they probably live through the winter in the perfect state, concealed under fallen leaves and rubbish on the surface of the ground. Fumigation with tobacco, and the application of a solution of whale-oil soap in water with a syringe, is the best means for destroying these leaf-hoppers."

We have enumerated but a very small part of the numerous insects which infest the rose, and in the absence of correct information on this important branch of floriculture, it is much to be hoped that farther investigations will be made by men of leisure. As an instance of the great variety of these insects, a French writer remarks that he "found in less than an hour, on the leaves of two species only of the Rose, six kinds of small caterpillars, all differing from each other in the number of their feet, the color of their head and body, and the lines and points with which they were marked. Their habits were all apparently the same. They lived between two or three folds which they had secured in shape by the films of their silk. Thus enveloped and protected, they eat the leaf until it is wholly or at least partly consumed. They then endeavor to establish themselves on another leaf, in which also they enwrap themselves, and consume it in the same manner. The plants attacked by these caterpillars are known by their ruffled leaves, partly eaten, and more or less covered with silk." The writer does not give their name, nor the result of any experiments for their destruction; he merely mentions it as an instance of the great abundance of insects on almost every plant. Such being the case, there is abundant room for farther observation and research.

HISTORY OF THE ROSE.

"Round every flower there gleams a glory,
Bequeathed by antique song or story;
To each old legends give a name,
And its peculiar charm proclaim.
O'er smiling lawn, through shady grove,
Our dreaming poets pensive rove,
And strive to read their language rare,
And learn the lesson latent there."

CHAPTER X.

THE EARLY HISTORY OF THE ROSE, AND FABLES RESPECTING ITS ORIGIN.

Very little is known of the early history of the Rose, or who were its first cultivators; and on this point all is conjecture. Mention of it is made in the ancient Coptic manuscripts, while nothing concerning it can be distinguished, with any degree of certainty, on the Egyptian monuments which are left us. Bocastre, the French traveler, observes that he carefully searched all the monuments in Egypt, and could find neither sculpture nor painting, figure nor hieroglyphic, that would lead us to suppose that the Rose was cultivated by the ancient Egyptians. We are, however, induced to believe that this beautiful flower was known to them, from the fact that several varieties are now found in Egypt. Dr. Delile, Director of the Botanic Garden at Montpelier, and with whom we enjoyed some pleasant intercourse during a visit to that place, was with Napoleon in his expedition to Egypt. In his valuable published account of that expedition, he mentions that he found there two Roses—*Rosa alba*, and *Rosa centifolia;* and there is also reason to believe, that under Domitian the Egyptians cultivated another—*Rosa bifera.* It is quite probable that the Rose was planted in the celebrated gardens of Babylon, the formation of which is attributed to Semiramis, about 1200 years before the Christian era; and it also appears probable, from the testimony of modern travelers, that several kinds of roses crossed over into Persia.

It is very certain that the Rose was cultivated by the Jews during the reign of Solomon, about two centuries after Semiramis; for mention of this flower is made in the Scripture books attributed to that king. In the Song of Solomon, he says: "I am the Rose of Sharon, and the Lily of the valleys;" and in the Apocryphal Wisdom of Solomon—"Let us crown ourselves with rose-buds before they be withered."

It also appears, by several passages of the Book of Ecclesiasticus, the author of which lived about 700 years after Solomon, that the Jews possessed beautiful gardens of roses, particularly at Jericho. "I was exalted like a palm-tree in Engaddi, and as a rose-plant in Jericho:" xxiv. 14. "Hearken unto me, ye holy children, and bud forth as a rose growing by the brook of the field:" xxxix. 13. "And as the flower of roses in the spring of the year:" l. 8. These passages prove that this most fertile and beautiful portion of Palestine abounded in roses, palms, and cedars. They no longer, however, abound; for while "the cedars wave on Lebanon," and the solitary palm stands in its isolated beauty, the Rose has entirely disappeared; and that now called the Rose of Jericho is but a little plant of the family of *Cruciferæ.* The Greeks cultivated the Rose at an early period, during the time of Homer, who lived about 200 years after the wise Hebrew monarch. In the Iliad and Odyssey he borrows the brilliant colors of the Rose to paint the rising of the sun. Aurora, according to this poet, has fingers of roses, and perfumes the air with roses. Few poets are more celebrated than Homer for beauty of conception, and for his frequent similes borrowed from natural objects. His selection, in this instance, evinces that the Rose was neither an unknown nor an unadmired flower. Herodotus, who lived about 400 years before the Christian era, mentions that in Macedonia, in the gardens which were supposed to have belonged to Midas, there were roses of sixty petals, which grew spontaneously without culture, and emitted a most delightful perfume.

Ancient writings are full of allusions to the Rose, and fabulous accounts of its origin. From its brilliant colors, melting into each other as the shades of night melt into the glowing richness of the rising sun, it was frequently consecrated to Aurora. It was also consecrated to Harpocrates, the patron of Silence, of which it was considered the symbol. Thus the expression, "*sub rosa*" (under the Rose), signified that all that was said should remain secret; and there is scarcely used a more expressive device for a seal than the simple figure of a Rose. It was the custom, in some of the northern countries, to suspend a Rose over the table in the dining-room, reminding the guests that silence should be observed respecting all that might be said during the meal.

Anacreon, Bion, Theocritus, Apollodorus, and others, relate various fables respecting its origin, and its obtaining the bright color for which it is distinguished.

One fable relates that Flora, having found the dead body of one of her favorite nymphs, whose beauty could only be equaled by her virtue, implored the assistance of all the Olympian deities to aid her in changing it into a flower, which all others should acknowledge to be their queen. Apollo lent the vivifying power of his beams, Bacchus bathed it in nectar, Vertumnus gave its perfume,

Pomona its fruit, and Flora herself gave its diadem of flowers. A beetle is often represented on antique gems as expiring, surrounded by roses; and this is supposed to be an emblem of luxurious enervation; the beetle being said to have such an antipathy to roses, that the smell of them will cause its death.

From the earliest period the Greeks gave to the Rose the preference over all other plants, and distinguished it as the "Queen of Flowers." In the fragments which still exist of Sappho, who lived about 600 years before the Christian era, there are lines in which the Rose is placed in the highest rank.

Since Sappho, many poets, both ancient and modern, have celebrated in their songs the charming qualities of the Rose. They have chosen it for an emblem of the most beautiful things—for the most pleasing and delightful comparisons; and they have united in making it the symbol of innocence, of modesty, of grace, and of beauty. Quite a volume might be collected of all the verses and pleasant sentences that have been inspired by the elegant form of the Rose, its charming color, and delightful fragrance. Some of these we have inserted in another part of the work. Nothing proves better the preference which has always existed for this beautiful flower than the thoughts expressed by Sappho. Anacreon and the other poets of antiquity have since imitated her in almost every language, and the lines of these have sacrificed nothing of her elegance and freshness.

The poets and writers of the East have abundantly celebrated in their works the beauties of the Rose. According to the Boun-Dehesch, of Zoroaster, the stem of that flower was free from thorns until the entrance of Ahrimanus (the evil one) into the world; the universal spirit of evil, according to their doctrine, affecting not only man, but also the inferior animals, and even the very trees and plants. The same work states that every flower is appropriated to a particular angel, and that the hundred-leaved Rose (*Rosa centifolia*) is consecrated to an archangel of the highest order. Basil, one of the early fathers, had undoubtedly seen these passages in oriental works, when he related that at the creation of the world the Rose had no thorns, and that it was gradually furnished with them as mankind became more corrupt.

The oriental writers also represent the nightingale as sighing for the love of the Rose; and many beautiful stanzas have arisen from this fable. According to the *Language of Flowers;* "In a curious fragment by the celebrated Persian poet, Attar, entitled *Bulbul Nameh*, the Book of the Nightingale, all the birds appear before Solomon, and charge the nightingale with disturbing their rest by the broken and plaintive strains which he warbles forth all the night in a sort of frenzy and intoxication. The nightingale is summoned, questioned, and acquitted by the wise king; because the bird assures him that his vehement love for the Rose drives him to distraction, and causes him to break forth into those passionate and touching complaints which are laid to his charge." The same work also mentions that the Persians assert that "the nightingale, in spring, flutters around the rose-bushes, uttering incessant complaints, till, overpowered by the strong scent, he drops stupefied on the ground." The invention of these fables, extravagant as they are, evince the Persian fondness for this beautiful flower. The Ghebers, or Persian fire-worshipers, believe that Abraham was thrown into the fire by Nimrod, when the flame turned into a bed of roses. According to the Hindoo mythology, Pagoda Siri, one of the wives of Vishnu, was found in a rose.

Among the many stories of roses in the East, is that of the philosopher Zeb, related by Madame de Latour. "There was at Amadan, in Persia, an academy with the following rules: Its members must think much write a little, and be as silent as possible. The learned Zeb, celebrated through all the East, learning that there was a vacancy in the academy, endeavored to obtain it, but arrived, unfortunately, too late. The academy was annoyed because it had given to power what belonged to merit; and the president, not knowing how to express a refusal without mortifying the assembly, caused a cup to be brought, which he filled so full of water, that a single drop more would have made it run over. The wise philosopher understood by that emblem that no place remained for him, and was retiring sadly, when he perceived a rose petal at his feet. At that sight he took courage, seized the petal, and placed it so delicately on the water, that not a single drop escaped. At this ingenious allusion to the rules of the academy, the whole assembly clapped their hands, and the philosopher was admitted as a member." Madame de Genlis relates very nearly the same anecdote, but attributes it to Abdul-kadri, a person celebrated among the Turks, who was desirous of residing at Babylon, where they were unwilling to receive him.

The Turks themselves, matter-of-fact as they are, have also seen something marvelous in the beautiful and vivid tints which the hand of nature has painted on the corolla of the Rose; but their imagination, less glowing than that of the Greeks, furnished them an idea more singular than pleasing. They suppose that the Rose owed its origin to the perspiration which fell from Mahomet; for which reason they never tread upon a rose-leaf, or suffer one to lie on the ground.

Meshilu, the Turkish poet, speaks of "a pavilion of roses as the seat of pleasure raised in the garden;" of "roses like the bright cheeks of beautiful maidens;" of the time when "the plants were sick, and the rose-bud hung its thoughtful head on its bosom;" and of the "dew, as it falls, being changed into rose-water." They also sculpture a rose on the tombstone of a female who dies unmarried.

The early Roman Catholics have made the Rose the subject of various miraculous events, one of which is attributed to the canonized Elizabeth, Queen of Hungary. As the French author, Montalembert, relates it in his history of that Queen, Elizabeth loved to carry to the poor herself, by stealth, not only money, but even food, and other things which she had provided for them. She went thus loaded, and on foot, by the steep and hidden paths which led from the chateau to the town, and to the cottages in the neighboring valleys. One day, when, accompanied by her favorite maid, she was descending by a rough and scarcely visible path, carrying under her cloak some bread, meat, eggs, and other food, for distribution among the poor, she was suddenly met by her husband, who was returning from the chase. Astonished to see her thus bending under the weight of her burden, he said to her, "Let me see what you are carrying." At the same time he threw open the cloak, which she held, with terror, to her breast, but found, as the legend says, nothing there but some white and red roses, the most beautiful he had ever seen.

D'Orbessan, in his work on the Rose, states, that in the church of Sainte-Luzanne, at Rome, is a mosaic of the time of Charlemagne, in which that prince is represented in a square mantle, and on his knees, while St. Peter is placing in his hands a standard covered with roses.

Michaud, in his *Biographie Universelle*, speaks of Clemence Isaure, a French lady, who lived in the latter part of the fifteenth century. She bequeathed to the academy of Toulouse a large income, exclusively for the celebration of floral games, and for the distribution of five prizes for as many pieces of poetry. The prizes consisted of an amaranth and rose of gold, and of a violet, marigold, and lily, of silver. The will also required that every three years, on the day of the commencement of the floral games, among other ceremonies to be observed, the members of the academy should visit and spread flowers upon her tomb. Ronsard, the French poet, having gained the first prize in the floral games, received, in place of the accustomed rose, a silver image of Minerva. Mary, Queen of Scots, was so much delighted with Ronsard's beautiful poetry on the Rose, that she sent him a magnificent rose of silver, valued at £500, with this inscription:—"*A. Ronsard. l'Apollon de la source des Muses.*"

CHAPTER XI.

LUXURIOUS USE OF THE ROSE.

The ancients possessed, at a very early period, the luxury of roses, and the Romans brought it to perfection by covering with beds of these flowers the couches whereon their guests were placed, and even the tables which were used for banquets;* while some emperors went so far as to scatter them in the halls of their palaces. At Rome, they were, at one time, brought from Egypt in that part of the year when Italy could not produce them; but afterwards, in order to render these luxuries more easily attainable during the winter by the leaders of the *ton* in that capital city of the world's empire, their gardeners found the means of producing, in green-houses warmed by means of pipes filled with hot water, an artificial temperature, which kept roses and lilies in bloom until the last of the year. Seneca declaimed, with a show of ridicule, against these improvements;† but, without being discouraged by the reasoning of the philosopher, the Romans carried their green-houses to such perfection that, at length, during the reign of Domitian, when the Egyptians thought to pay him a splendid compliment in honor of his birthday, by sending him roses in the midst of winter, their present excited nothing but ridicule and disdain, so abundant had winter roses become at Rome by the efforts of art. Few of the Latin poets have been

* "Tempora subtilius pinguntur tecta coronis,
Et latent injecta splendida mensa Rosa." (OVID, lib. v.)

† "Non vivunt contra naturam, qui hieme concupiscunt Rosam? Fomentoque aquarum calentium, et calorum apta imitatione, bruma lilium florem vernum, exprimunt." (*Seneca, epistle* 122-8.)

more celebrated for their epigrammatic wit than Martial; and his epigram "To Cæsar, on the Winter Roses," serves to show that the culture of roses at Rome was carried to such perfection as to make the attempts of foreign competitors subjects only for ridicule.

"The ambitious inhabitants of the land watered by the Nile have sent thee, O Cæsar, the roses of winter, as a present valuable for its novelty. But the boatman of Memphis will laugh at the gardens of Pharaoh as soon as he has taken one step in thy capital city—for the spring, in its charms, and the flowers in their fragrance and beauty, equal the glory of the fields of Pæstum. Wherever he wanders or casts his eyes, every street is brilliant with garlands of roses. And thou, O Nile, must now yield to the fogs of Rome. Send us thy harvests, and we will send thee roses."

By this passage it is evident that the cultivation of Roses among the ancients was much farther advanced than is generally supposed. In another epigram Martial speaks again of roses, which were formerly seen only in the spring, but which, in his time, had become common during the winter. We are, also, but copyists of the Romans in the cultivation of flowers in windows; for vases of every style of beauty, and filled with roses, were a frequent ornament of their windows. Martial says that a miserly patron had made him a present of a very small estate, and adds that he has a much better country place in his window. Much that illustrates the use which the ancients made of roses in their ceremonies, in their festivals, and in their domestic life, may be found in various authors, evincing still more how very common the use of them had become. Florus relates that Antiochus, king of Syria, being encamped in the island of Eubœa, under woven tents of silk and gold, was not only accompanied by a band of musicians, but that he might yet more enhance his pleasures, he wished to procure roses; and although it was in the midst of winter, he caused them to be collected from every quarter.

The gallants of Rome were in the habit of presenting their favorite damsels with the first roses that appeared in spring; and "*Mea rosa*" was an affectionate expression they often used to their betrothed.

We frequently find in old Latin authors an entire abandonment to pleasure and excessive luxury, signified by such expressions as "living in the midst of roses," "sleeping on roses," etc. ("*Vivere in rosa,*" "*dormire in rosa.*")

Seneca speaks of Smyndiride, the most wealthy and voluptuous of the Sybarites, who could not sleep if a single one of the rose-petals with which his bed was spread, happened to be curled.

Cicero, in his "*De finibus,*" alludes to the custom which prevailed at Rome at that time, of reclining at the table on couches covered with roses; and comparing the happiness which virtue gives to the pleasures of luxury says, that "Regulus, in his chains, was more happy than Thorius drinking on a couch of roses, and living in such a manner that one could scarcely imagine any rare and exquisite pleasure of which he did not partake."

The same author, in his celebrated speech against Verres, the greatest extortioner whose name is recorded in history, reproached him not only with the outrageous robberies and cruelties which he committed during the three years that he was governor of Sicily, but yet more with his effeminacy and licentiousness. "When spring commenced," said the Roman orator, "that season was not announced to him by the return of Zephyr, nor by the appearance of any heavenly sign; it was not until he had seen the roses bloom that spring was visible to his voluptuous eye. In the voyages which he made across the province, he was accustomed, after the example of the kings of Bithynia, to be carried in a litter borne by eight men, in which he reposed, softly extended upon cushions made of transparent material, and filled with roses of Malta, having in his hand a net of the finest linen, and equally full of these flowers, whose fragrance incessantly gratified his eager nostrils."

Latinus Pacatus, in his eulogium on the Emperor Theodosius, inveighs against the luxury of the Romans, whose sensual desires, he says, were not satisfied until they had reversed the order of the seasons, and produced roses in the winter season to crown their cup of wine, and until their Falernian, during the summer, was cooled in large vessels filled with ice. The forcing of roses in winter is no longer extensively practiced in Rome; but during the summer they are abundant, and we recollect being much struck with admiration of some beautiful hedges of the Daily rose in the villas near Rome.

After reading the preceding statements of the abundance of roses among the ancient Romans, it is with some surprise that we recollect the great scarcity of that flower during the gayest and most animated festival of the modern Romans—the Carnival. As we slowly walked along the Corso, submitting with as quiet a grace as possible to the various fantastic tricks of the masked figures around us, and occasionally pelted with handfuls of sugar-plums from the windows, or passing carriages, we looked in vain for roses or camellias in the numerous bouquets that were cleaving the air around us. Little bouquets of violets were numerous, and the air was thick with them, as our eyes, nose, and mouth, could bear striking witness; and we recollect, too, the contemptuous curl of the lip, and rush of the aristocratic blood into the face of a fair English girl in one of the carriages whose blue eyes had been nearly closed by an awkward cast of one of these little bouquets from the hand of a plebian performer. But we only recollect catching a glimpse now and then of a *single* rose or camellia, skillfully passed by a cavalier below into the hands of some dark-eyed beauty in the balconies above, the bright sparkle of whose eye convinced us that the single flower was of value, and a mark of especial regard. The Rose appeared to be valued as some rare exotic, and not to be idly bestowed where there was small probability of its due appreciation; it was, indeed, a "*rara flora in urbe*," and quite superseded by the very pretty and abundant violets.

The modern Romans have not only lost many of the good qualities of their early ancestors, but they have also escaped much of the effeminate softness which characterized the Romans under some of the later emperors; and, as belonging to this state of luxury, the cultivation of the Rose has, in modern times, been much neglected. The homage of the Romans is now reserved for art, and the beautiful products of nature are, in their opinion, worthy only of secondary consideration. The Rose is now mostly confined in that city to the residences of the wealthier classes, and can scarcely be said to have resumed its old place in Roman esteem until it is again a favorite with the mass of the people.

When Cleopatra went into Cilicia to meet Mark Antony, she gave him, for several successive days, festivals in which she displayed a truly royal magnificence. She caused to be placed in the banqueting hall twelve couches, each of which would hold three guests. The walls were covered with purple tapestry, interwoven with gold; all the vases were of gold, admirably executed, and enriched with precious stones.

On the fourth day, the queen carried her sumptuousness so far as to pay a talent (about six hundred dollars) for a quantity of roses, with which she caused the floor of the hall to be covered to the depth of eighteen inches. These flowers were retained by a very fine net, in order that the guests might walk over them.

After the loss of the battle of Actium, Antony, not wishing to survive his defeat, from fear of falling into the hands of Augustus, thrust himself through with his sword, and requested Cleopatra to scatter perfumes over his tomb, and to cover it with roses.

The greatest profusion of roses mentioned in ancient history, and which is scarcely credible, is that which Suetonius attributes to Nero. This author says, that at a fête which the emperor gave in the Gulf of Baiæ, when inns were established on the banks, and ladies of distinction played the part of hostesses, the expense incurred for roses alone was more than four millions of sesterces—about $100,000. Since Nero, many of his successors have nearly equaled him in prodigal enjoyment of the luxury of roses. Lucius Aurelius Verus, whose licentiousness and destitution of every manly quality equaled that of the worst emperors, but whom no one reproaches with any act of cruelty, was the inventor of a new species of luxury. He had a couch made on which were four raised cushions, closed on all sides by a very thin net, and filled with leaves of roses. Heliogabalus, celebrated for luxury and vice of every kind, caused roses to be crushed with the kernels of the pine (Pinus maritima), in order to increase the perfume. The same emperor caused roses to be scattered over the couches, the halls, and even the porticoes of the palace, and he renewed this profusion with flowers of every kind—lilies, violets, hyacinths, narcissus, etc. Gallien, another equally cruel and luxurious prince, lay, according to some authors, under arbors of roses; and, according to others, on beds covered with these flowers. And finally, Carrius, another licentious and prodigal emperor, who reigned only a few months, caused roses to be scattered over the chambers of his palace, and on the couches of his guests.

CHAPTER XII.

THE ROSE, IN CEREMONIES AND FESTIVALS, AND IN THE ADORNMENT OF BURIAL-PLACES.

Among the ancients, the Rose was conspicuous in all the sacred ceremonies, and in public and private fêtes. The Greeks and the Romans surrounded the statues of Venus, of Hebe, and of Flora, with garlands of roses. They were lavish of these flowers at the festivals of Flora; in those of Juno, at Argos, the statue of the Olympian Queen was crowned with lilies and roses. In the festivals of Hymen, at Athens, the youth of both sexes, crowned with roses and adorned with flowers, mingled in dances which were intended to represent the innocence of primeval times. At Rome, in the public rejoicings, they sometimes strewed the streets with roses and other flowers. It is thus that Lucretius gives a description of the manner in which were celebrated the festivals of Cybele.*

To scatter flowers on the passage of the funeral procession of a private citizen was an honor not common at Rome. Pliny informs us, however, that a Scipio, belonging to the illustrious family of that name, who while he was tribune, fulfilled his duties to the satisfaction of the people, dying without leaving sufficient to pay his funeral expenses, the people voluntarily contributed to pay them, and on the appearance of the body, cast flowers upon its passage.

---

* "Ergo cum primum, magnas invecta per urbes
Munificat tacita mortales muta salute;
Ære atque argento, sternunt iter omne viarum.
Largifica stipe dilantes, ninguntque Rosarum
Floribus, umbrantes matrem comitumque catervas."

LUCRETIUS, lib. ii., ver. 625.

At Baiæ, when fêtes were given upon the water, the whole surface of the lake of Lucina appeared covered with roses.

The custom of encircling the head, of surrounding the neck, and also the breast, with crowns and garlands of roses, on different occasions, and particularly during the last days of a gay festival, when, after the solid dishes, they passed to the dessert and the rare wines, is well known by the odes of Anacreon, and from the writings of several of the ancient poets.

The voluptuous Horace, when he abandoned himself to pleasures, was always supplied with roses. In congratulating one of his friends on his safe return from Spain, he recommended that these flowers should not be wanting at the festival. On another occasion, he told his favorite servant that he cordially disliked the pompous displays of the Persians, and escaped them by searching in what place the late Rose was found. Drawing a picture of luxurious ease for his friend Hirpinus, he speaks of "lying under the shade of a lofty Plane or Pine tree, perfuming our spotless hair with Assyrian spikenard, and crowning ourselves with roses." We can very well judge how general had become the custom of making crowns of roses, from the number of times which it is mentioned in Pliny, and the frequency with which Martial speaks of it in his epigrams. The latter author also informs us, that in the very height of Roman luxury and reveling, the most favorable time for soliciting and obtaining a favor was when the patron was entirely given up to the pleasures of the table and of roses.*

Whatever doubt may exist of the use of crowns of roses, as objects of luxury, it is well authenticated, that

* "Hæc hora est tua, dum furit Lyæus
Cum regnat Rosa, cum madent capilli,
Tunc me vel rigidi legant Catones."
Lib. x., epig. 19.

among medical men of antiquity, endeavors were made to determine what kinds of flowers were suitable to place in crowns without detriment to health; and according to the report made on this subject, the parsley, the ivy, the myrtle, and the Rose, possessed peculiar virtues for dissipating the fumes of the wine. According to Athenæus, a crown of roses possessed not only the property of alleviating pain in the head, but had a very refreshing effect.

Pliny mentions two Greek physicians—Mnesitheus and Callimachus,—who wrote on this subject.

The custom of crowning with roses had passed from the Greeks to the Romans, and it also existed among the Hebrews, who had probably borrowed it from some of the neighboring nations, either from the Egyptians, in the midst of whom they had spent many years, or from the Babylonians, with whom they had in the captivity much connection. The practice of this custom among the Israelites is attested by the previously quoted passage, in the apocryphal "Wisdom of Solomon."

At Rome it was not only at the religious festivals that they crowned themselves with roses and other flowers, but it was the custom to wear these crowns during public and private fêtes; they were strictly forbidden at some other times, and above all on certain public occasions, where to appear with such an ornament would pass for an insult to a public calamity. Pliny informs us, that during the second Punic war, which lasted sixteen years, a banker named Lucius Fulvius, for looking from his gallery on the Forum, and wearing a crown of roses on his head, was, by order of the Senate, sent to prison, from which he was not liberated until the end of the war.

This anecdote, moreover, proves that crowns of roses were in fashion at Rome at an early period, and before licentiousness and luxury had yet made many inroads upon the national character.

It may readily be supposed, that at Rome, under the

emperors, the use of crowns of flowers was, like every other species of luxury at that time, constantly on the increase. At first they wore the crowns interwoven with leaves of flowers, then they wore them composed partly of roses, and finally they were not satisfied unless they consisted of these flowers only.

Martial, as we have already mentioned, speaks often of his crowns of roses. The crown sent by this poet to his friend Sabinus was composed entirely of these flowers, and he was desirous that they should be considered the production of his own gardens.

From the poverty of Turkish history, little is known of the early use of the Rose among them. We have, however, some account of its use among the Mohammedan Persians.

Although wine was forbidden by the laws of Mahomet, the Persians frequently made use of it; and in the time of Tavernier and of Chardin, they frequently drank it to excess. One of their kings, Soliman III., was intoxicated almost every day; and it was the custom then in Persia, to serve the wine in crystal decanters, which, when the season permitted, they corked with roses.

The most interesting purpose to which roses were devoted was the adornment of tombs and burial-places. The Greeks employed generally for this object, the myrtle and the amaranth; but the Romans gave the preference to the lily, the saffron-plant, and, above all, the Rose.

The ancients were careful to renew the plants which were placed around the sepulchral urn, in order that it might be surrounded by a continual spring. These flowers were regarded as sacred, and as a relic of the deceased.

The Romans considered this pious care so agreeable to the spirits of the departed, that wealthy citizens bequeathed by will entire gardens, to be reserved for furnishing their tombs with flowers. They also often ordered that their heirs, or those to whom they left a legacy for the care of their ashes, should meet together every year, on the anniversary of their death, and dine near their tomb, scattering roses about the place. This custom is attested by several stories of ancient Roman tombs. One with an ancient inscription was found at Ravenna, and others in some other parts of Italy.

D'Orbessan, in his "*Essai sur les Roses*," mentions having seen, at Torcello, a city about five miles from Venice, an inscription of this kind, mentioning a donation made by an emancipated slave to the assembly of the *Centum*, consisting of gardens and a building to be employed in celebrating his obsequies and those of his master. It requested that roses should not be spared, and that food should be then distributed in abundance. Generally, the donation made on condition of covering the funeral monument with roses was transferred to another, if that condition was not fulfilled. Sometimes the most terrible maledictions threatened those who dared to violate these sacred gardens. That which proves how frequent among the Romans was this custom of ornamenting tombs with roses is, that those who were not rich enough to make such bequests often directed to be engraved upon the stone which covered their remains a request to the passers-by to scatter roses upon their tomb. Some of these stones still exist, with the following inscription: "*Sparge, precor, Rosas supra mea busta, viator.*" It was, perhaps, because they compared the short duration of human life to the quick fading existence of the Rose, that this flower was devoted to the burial-place of the dead; and there can certainly be chosen no more beautiful emblem of this transitory state of existence. This supposition is somewhat strengthened by the following passage from Jerome, one of the early Christian fathers:

"The ancients scattered roses over the urns of the deceased, and in their wills ordered that these flowers should adorn their graves, and should be renewed every year. It was also the custom for husbands to cast roses, violets, and lilies, on the urns which enclosed the ashes of their wives. These modest flowers were emblematic signs of their grief. Our Christians were content to place a Rose among the ornaments of their graves, as the image of life."

In Turkey, females that died unmarried had a rose sculptured at the top of their monument.

At the well-known cemetery of Père la Chaise, which has often excited the ecstasy, admiration, or praise of many travelers, but which in reality exhibits neither elegance, sentiment, nor taste, wreaths of roses and other flowers are frequently seen upon the thickly crowded tombs, either as mementos of affection, or in compliance with a popular custom; while the street leading to the cemetery is filled with shops in which are exposed for sale the wreaths of flowers.

The prevalence of the same custom in Denmark is alluded to by Shakespeare, in Hamlet, in the scene of Ophelia's burial.

The custom still remains also in America and Great Britain. In Wales, when a young girl dies, her female companions bring flowers with them to her funeral, and place them in her coffin. They plant lilies and snow-drops over the graves of children, and wild and cultivated roses over those of adults.

Gwillym, a Welsh poet, thus speaks of the custom in one of his elegies:—"Oh! while the season of flowers and the tender sprays, thick of leaves, remain, I will pluck the roses from the brakes, to be offered to the memory of a child of fairest fame; humbly will I lay them on the grave of Ivor."

Evelyn tells us that "the white rose was planted at the grave of a virgin, and her chaplet was tied with white riband, in token of her spotless innocence; though sometimes black ribands were intermingled, to bespeak the grief of the survivors. The red rose was occasionally used in remembrance of such as had been remarkable for their benevolence; but roses in general were appropriated to the graves of lovers."

Drummond, the Scotch poet, requested one of his friends to have the following couplet placed over his grave:

> "Here Damon lies, whose songs did sometimes grace
> The murmuring Esk:—may roses shade the place."

The first Christians disapproved of the use of these flowers, either at their festivals or as ornaments for their tombs, on account of its connection with the pagan mythology, and the custom thus became extinct. Tertullian wrote a book against crowns and garlands. Clement of Alexandria thought it improper that Christians should crown themselves with roses. A little later, however, Christians relaxed from this strictness, and the Christian poet Prudence did not fear to invite his brethen "to cover with violets and with verdure, and to surround with perfumes those bones which the voice of the All-Powerful would one day restore to life."

The Roman Catholics of this day admit flowers to their churches and ceremonies, and on feast days they adorn the altars with bouquets and garlands. At the most imposing of these solemnities, the day of the "*Fête-Dieu*," rose petals, during the procession, are scattered in the air, and blended with the perfume of censers, directed towards the Host; in many of the towns, particularly those in the south of France and of Europe, the streets through which the procession passes are scattered throughout with fragrant herbs and flowers of every kind.

Since the extinction of paganism in a greater part of the world, the custom of wearing crowns of flowers at festivals has passed entirely away. Women only use roses as an ornament for their hair, or employ them in different parts of their toilet. In our own country the toilet of a bride is never considered perfect unless she wears a wreath of roses or other flowers, whose snow-white hue is an emblem of her departing maidenhood. Sometimes she is provided only with a bouquet of white roses and camellias, and her bridesmaids wear similar ornaments of nature's manufacture.

The Rose is abundantly used by children in their beautiful celebration of May-day. We well recollect our enjoyment of one of these scenes some years since. We were returning from a ride in the vicinity of Charleston, S. C., on the first day of this, the sunniest of the months of spring—a day dedicated not to the spirit of motion, and celebrated not by processions of furniture carts, amid the bustle and noise of a populous city, but dedicated there, at the sunny South, to innocent and joyous festivity, and celebrated amid all the fresh and fragrant luxuriance of southern vegetation, surrounded by the delicate sweetness of the magnolia, the Rose, and other flowers, while the mocking-bird, with its sweet and varied note, was the minstrel for the occasion. Riding quietly along the road, we were suddenly stopped by a procession which had just dismounted from a number of carriages in a beautiful grove hard by. It consisted mostly of noble-looking boys and beautiful girls, of all ages under fourteen, the latter dressed in white and crowned with wreaths of roses and other flowers. The manly attention of the boys to the fair creatures with whom they walked hand in hand would not have disgraced the gallantry of Bayard, or the politeness of Chesterfield. As the procession wound slowly from our view, under the shade of the lofty live oak and the rich magnolia, we could not help reflecting how beautiful was this graceful enjoyment of the sunny days of childhood, and how preferable to the mental excitement and precocious training of many of the infant philosophers of this most enlightened nineteenth century.

It is much to be regretted that in circles where fashion reigns supreme, nature is gradually giving way to art, and instead of the fresh and natural beauty of a newly gathered Rose, various forms of artificial flowers are found upon the center table, or in the hair of those whose quick discernment and refined taste should lead them to perceive the great inferiority of these artificial toys to the delicate beauty and welcome fragrance of a Rose just from its parent plant.

Very much additional matter could be inserted respecting the early history of the Rose, and its connection with ancient superstitions. Sufficient, however, has been given to show the esteem in which the Rose was held by the ancient Greeks and Romans.

CHAPTER XIII.

THE ROSE IN THE MIDDLE AGES.

In Great Britain, according to Loudon, "one of the earliest notices of the Rose occurs in Chaucer, who wrote early in the 13th century; and in the beginning of the 15th century, there is evidence of the Rose having been cultivated for commercial purposes, and of the water distilled from it being used to give a flavor to a variety of dishes, and to wash the hands at meals—a custom still preserved in some of the colleges, and also in many of the public halls within the city of London."

In 1402, Sir William Clopton granted to Thomas Smyth a piece of ground called Dokmedwe, in Haustede, for the annual payment of a rose to Sir William and his heirs, in lieu of all services. The demand for roses formerly was so great, that bushels of them were frequently paid by vassals to their lords, both in England and France. The single rose, paid as an acknowledgment, was the diminutive representation of a bushel of roses—as a single peppercorn, which is still a reserved rent, represents a pound of peppercorns — a payment originally of some worth, but descending by degrees to a mere formality. Among the new-year gifts presented to Queen Mary in 1556, was a bottle of rose-water; and in 1570 we find, among the items in the account of a dinner of Lord Leicester, when he was Chancellor of the University of Oxford, three ounces of rose-water. In an account of a grant of a great part of Ely House, Holborne, by the Bishop of Ely, to Christopher Hatton, for twenty-one years, the tenant covenants to pay, on midsummer-day, a red rose for the gate-house and garden, and for the ground (fourteen acres) ten loads of hay and £10 per annum; the Bishop reserving to himself and successors free access through the gate-house, for walking in the gardens and gathering twenty bushels of roses yearly. In 1597, we find Gerard speaking of the Damask rose of Damascus and the Cinnamon rose as common in English gardens. Hakluyt says that the rose of Damascus was brought to England by De Linaker, physician to Henry IX.; and his successor, Sir Richard Weston, who wrote in 1645, says, "We have red roses from France." In the reign of James I., the keeper of the robes and jewels at Whitehall, among a variety of other offices, had separate salaries allowed him, "for fire to air the hot-houses, 40s. by the year;" and, "for digging and setting of roses, in the spring gardens, 40s. by the year."

It would seem, by these incidents, that previous to the seventeenth century, roses were far from being abundant, and indeed were so rare, that a bottle of distilled water was a fit present for Royalty, and a few roses an amply sufficient rent for house and land.

In the times of chivalry, the Rose was often an emblem that knights were fond of placing in their helmet or shield, implying that sweetness should always be the companion of courage, and that beauty was the only prize worthy of valor. It was not, however, always taken for such emblems, nor did it always bring to mind pleasant and agreeable images, but was often the signal for bloodshed in a desolating civil war which raged in England for more than thirty years.

The rival factions of the *White* and the *Red* Rose arose in 1452, during the reign of Henry VI., between the houses of Lancaster and of York. The Duke of York, a descendant of Edward III., claimed that his house possessed a nearer title to the crown than the reigning branch. He adopted a *white* rose on his shield, for his device, and the reigning monarch, Henry VI., of the house of Lancaster, carried the *red* rose. After several furious civil wars, after having flooded the whole kingdom with blood, and after the tragical death of three kings, Henry VII., of the house of Lancaster, re-united, in 1486, the two families by marrying Elizabeth, the heiress of the house of York.

The adoption of the red rose, by the house of Lancaster, was at a period far prior to these civil wars. About 1277, the Count of Egmont, son of the King of England, and who had taken the title of Count of Champagne, was sent by the King of France to Provence, with some troops, to avenge the murder of William Pentecôte, mayor of the city, who had been killed in an insurrection.

When this prince returned into England, after executing his orders, he took for his device the red rose, that Thibaut, Count of Brie and of Champagne, had brought from Syria, on his return from the crusade some years before.—That Count of Egmont was the head of the house of Lancaster, who preserved the red rose on their arms, while the house of York, on the other hand, adopted the white rose as their device.

An anecdote is told of the Prince of Bearne, afterwards Henry IV. of France, who was not 15 years of age when

8*

Charles IX. came to Nerae, in 1566, to visit the court of Navarre.

The fifteen days that he spent there were marked by sports and fêtes, of which the young Henry was already the chief ornament. Charles IX. loved to practice archery; in providing for him that amusement, they thought that none of his courtiers, not even the Duke of Guise, who excelled at this sport, would venture to prove himself more adroit than the monarch. The young Henry, however, advanced, and at the first shot, carried off the orange, which served for a mark. According to the rules of the sport, he wished, as victor, to shoot first in the next trial; the King opposed it, and repulsed him with warmth; Henry stepped back a little, drew his bow, and directed the arrow against the breast of his adversary; the monarch quickly took shelter behind the largest of his courtiers, and requested them to take away "that dangerous little cousin." Peace being made, the same sport was continued on the following day; Charles found an excuse for not coming. This time the Duke of Guise carried away the orange, which he split in two, and no other could be found for a mark.

The young prince perceived a Rose in the bosom of a young girl among the spectators, and seizing it, quickly placed it on the mark. The Duke shot first, and missed; Henry succeeding him, placed his arrow in the middle of the flower, and returned it to the pretty villager with the victorious arrow which had pierced it.

At Salency, a village of France, the Rose is the reward of excellent traits of character; they attribute the origin of the fête of La Rosière, in that country, to Medard, bishop of Noyou, who lived at the end of the fifteenth, and beginning of the sixteenth century, during the reign of Clovis. That bishop, who was also Lord of Salency, had established a fund, giving a sum of twenty-five livres (five dollars), and a crown or hat of roses, to the young girl on his estate who enjoyed the greatest reputation for amiability and excellence of character. Tradition states that the prelate himself gave this desired prize to one of his sisters, whom the public voice had named to be Rosière. Before the revolution of 1789, there could be seen, beneath the altar of the chapel of St. Medard, at Salency, a tablet, where that bishop was represented in pontifical dress, and placing a crown of roses on the head of his sister, who was on her knees, with her hair dressed.

The bishop had set aside, on a part of his domain, since called the "Manor of the Rose," an annual rent of twenty-five livres, at that time a considerable sum, for paying all the expenses of this ceremony. It is stated that Louis XIII., being at the chateau of Varennes, near Salency, about the time of this ceremony, was deirous of adding to its *èclat* by his personal presence; but finding himself indisposed, he sent to La Rosière, by a marquis of rank and first captain of his guards, a ring and his blue ribbon. "Go," said he to the marquis, "and present this riband to her who shall be crowned. It has been long the prize of honor; it shall now become the reward of virtue." Since that time La Rosière has received a ring, and she and her companions have worn the blue ribbon.

The Lord of Salency at one time enjoyed the right of choosing La Rosière from three of the village girls, who were presented by the inhabitants. But in 1773 a new lord, who purchased the estate of Salency, wished to take away the right enjoyed by the inhabitants, of naming and presenting to him the three candidates for the Rose. He assumed the nomination of La Rosière, without any assembling, election, or presentation, and suppressed entirely the pomp and ceremonies which until that time had always been observed. On the complaint of the inhabitants of Salency, the Court of Chancery at once set aside the pretensions of their lord; but he, not wishing to yield them, instituted a civil process before the Parliament of

Paris, which gave a decree in favor of the inhabitants of the place, by which it confirmed to them all the ancient customs of the fête of La Rosière, of which the Lord of Salency was ordered to pay all the expenses.

The ceremony of La Rosière was suppressed during the excesses of the Revolution, but was reëstablished when the times had become more quiet. The celebration takes place in June, and would be well worthy the attendance of foreign travelers.

We have mentioned this custom very much in detail, as it is one of the few ceremonies still existing, in which the Rose occupies a prominent position, and is made alone the reward of merit. Other festivals of the Rose, similar to those of Salency, were established in several other villages of France and the neighboring countries. When Louis XVIII. was staying at Blakenbourg, in Germany, during the years of his exile, he was invited to assist at a festival of La Rosière. When he had placed the crown on the head of the young girl who was designated as the most virtuous, she said to him, ingenuously, "My Prince, may *your* crown be restored you."

There exists a touching custom in the valley of Engadine, in Switzerland. If a man accused of a crime is able to justify himself the same day on which he is liberated from prison, a young and beautiful girl offers him a white rose, called the Rose of Innocence.

It is somewhat singular that, although the Rose was in these instances employed as the emblem of virtue and innocence, it has been considered, at other times and places, as a sign of disgrace and dishonor.

The synod held at Nismes, about the year 1284, ordered the Jews to wear on their breast a rose, to distinguish them from Christians, in order that they might not receive the same attentions. At one time, in certain German provinces, a crown of red roses was the punishment of immorality.

It appears that, in the Middle Ages, roses were much more abundantly cultivated in certain provinces than they have been since; for the following passage is found in Marchangy's History of France in the 14th century: "For the ornament of certain festivals, they cultivate, in the vicinity of Rouen, fields of flowers of several rods; and the annual sale of bouquets and wreaths of roses is valued at 50,000 francs. The business of *maker of wreaths*, and that of *rose merchant*, is in France very common and very profitable. The above sum will not seem surprising, when we think of the enormous consumption of rose-water at that time. In all family parties, companies, and associations, many bouquets were presented; at table, during festivals, they crowned themselves with flowers, and scattered them on the table-cloth and the floor."

The Marquis de Chesnel, in his History of the Rose, mentions that, among the old customs of Auvergne, Anjou, Tours, Lodunois, and Maine, there was one in the noble families, that a father who had sons, frequently gave to his daughters, on their marriage, only a wreath of roses. In Normandy, also, the daughters received, for their legitimate portion, a hat adorned with the same flowers. Among the ancient seigniorial rights in France, in the 14th century, was one by which each tenant was obliged to furnish a bushel of roses for the manufacture of rose-water for the lord of the soil. Madame de Genlis mentions, however, that about the same period, every one was not allowed to cultivate these flowers; but permission to do so was granted to privileged persons. Whether it was ever a royal monopoly she does not state; but it would certainly be no more singular than the monopoly of the sale of butter by the King of Naples.

We have already mentioned the wars of the White and Red Rose, which during so long a time deluged England with blood. There is also an instance in French history, where this flower, associated as it is with innocence and pleasant thoughts, served, under the reign of Charles VI., as the rallying sign of the faction of Burgundy against that of Armagnac. The Parisians, urged by the agents of the Duke of Burgundy, established the order of St. André for their partisans, in order to manage them more easily; and the church of St. Eustache was chosen as their rendezvous. Each church member wore a crown of red roses, of which more than seven hundred were made in the space of twelve hours, and the flowers were sufficiently abundant to perfume the whole church.

According to an ancient custom, the dukes and peers of France were formerly obliged to present roses to the Parliament of Paris, at certain periods of its session. The peer who was chosen to do the honors of this ceremony caused all the chambers of Parliament to be scattered with roses, flowers, and fragrant herbs; and entertained at a splendid breakfast the presidents, councilors, and even the notaries and door-keepers of the court. He afterwards went into each chamber, accompanied by a page with a large silver basin, which contained as many bouquets of roses and other flowers as there were public officers, with an equal number of crowns composed of the same flowers. The Parliament also had its cultivator of roses, called the *Rosièr de la Cour*, from whom the peers could obtain the roses for their presents.

Under the reign of Francis I., in 1541, there was a dispute between the Duc de Montpensier and the Duc de Nevers respecting the presentage of the roses to Parliament. It was decided that the Duc de Montpensier, from his rank as prince of the blood, should be entitled to the first presentage. Among the princes of the royal family who submitted to this ceremony at later periods, are numbered the dukes of Vendome, Beaumont, Angouleme, and several other distinguished names. Henry IV., while only King of Navarre, proved to the procureurgeneral that neither he nor his predecessors had ever failed to perform that duty.

About the year 1631, there was published a very curious book on the Rose, by a German named Rosenberg. About 250 octavo pages are devoted entirely to the praise of the curative properties of the Rose in almost every known disease, making, in fact, this flower a universal panacea for the many ills to which flesh is heir. The author also claims for it supernatural qualities, particularly for driving away evil spirits. The work closes by asserting, as a positive fact, supported by several authorities which he quotes, the remarkable regeneration or resurrection of the Rose. He gives also the process of this reproduction, which is scarcely worth inserting here, being, like the story of the Phœnix, a fable engendered by superstition upon ignorance. It is somewhat surprising that this fable should have been very gravely reproduced, in a French work on the Rose, published in 1800. The author states that, "notwithstanding the many marvelous things which we already know respecting the improving, forcing, changing, and multiplying of roses, we have yet to describe the most surprising of all—that of its regeneration; or, in other words, the manner of reproducing that flower from its own ashes. This is called the *imperial secret*, because the Emperor Ferdinand III. purchased it of a foreign chemist, at a very high price." The conclusion is a rather amusing instance of Munchausenism in the 19th century. "Finally, all this material being placed in a glass vessel, with a certain quantity of pure dew, forms a blue powder, from which, when heat is applied, there springs a stem, leaves, and flowers, and a whole and perfect plant is formed from its own ashes."

It is difficult to credit the fact that, in any part of this enlightened age, an author could be found who would gravely and in sincerity advance such opinions and state such facts as the above; and it is but an additional proof, if such were wanting, that nothing can be advanced too monstrous or too incredible to be entirely without believers.

If the sight of roses, or their delicate fragrance, has been generally delightful and pleasing, there have also been those who could not endure them. Anne of Austria, wife of Louis XIII., of France, although otherwise very fond of perfumes, had such an antipathy to the rose, that she could not bear the sight of one even in a painting. The Duke of Guise had a still stronger dislike, for he always made his escape at the sight of a rose. Dr. Ladelius mentions a man who was obliged to become a recluse, and dared not leave his house, during the season of roses; because, if he happened to imbibe their fragrance, he was immediately seized with a violent cold in his head.

The odor of the rose, like that of many other flowers, has often occasioned serious injury, particularly in closed apartments; and persons to whose sensitive organizations the odor is disagreeable should not sleep with them in the chamber. Some authors of credibility mention instances of death caused by a large quantity of roses being left during the night in a sleeping apartment.

CHAPTER XIV.

PERFUMES OF THE ROSE..

At an early period in the cultivation of the Rose, and after its admission among the luxuries of the wealthy, human skill was exerted to extract its delightful perfume.

Several authors have considered the invention of the essence of the Rose very ancient, and have even traced it back as far as the siege of Troy. This, however, can scarcely be admitted, for nothing relating to the essence or essential oil of roses can be found in Homer, or in any other author for many subsequent years. The discovery of these valuable articles of commerce was made at a much later period. If the essential oil of roses had been known to the ancient Greeks or Romans, it would probably have been more particularly mentioned by Pliny, and the mode of preparation even would have been described. In speaking, however, of various perfumes, he says nothing of any distillation from the petals of the Rose, but simply mentions that, as early as the siege of Troy, the *expressed* juice of roses was known, and being mixed with a delicate oil, formed an agreeable perfume.

In speaking of artificial oils in general, Pliny also observes that the oil of roses was made by simply steeping the rose-petals in oil. According to the same author, oil was the body of nearly all the perfumes used at that day, and for a perfuming substance, roses were most frequently used, because they grew everywhere in the greatest abundance.

Perfumes of every kind were more abundantly used among the ancient Greeks and Romans than at the present day. Athenæus, in his *Feast of Wise Men*, states that nearly all of these were drawn from the Rose, and says that the most sweet were those of Cyrene, while those of Naples, Capua, and Faseoli were the best and most delightful of all.

This agrees with the subsequent researches made on the same subject by D'Orbessan. "The cities of Naples, Capua, and Preneste," says the latter, "obtained their roses from Campania, where there is yet a considerable tract of land, commonly called *Il mazzone delle Rose.*

"This field is sometimes called *Rosetinus*, on account of the prodigious quantity of roses which grow there without culture, and in greater abundance than in any other section of that country."

Athenæus states that the perfume of roses was frequently used in culinary preparations, and gives a curious receipt for a sort of *pot-pourri*, made by the cook of the King of Sicily. "This is what I call *potted roses*, and it is thus prepared: I first pound some of the most fragrant roses in a mortar; then I take the brains of birds and pigs, well boiled and stripped of every particle of meat; I then add the yolks of some eggs, some oil, a little cordial, some pepper, and some wine: after having beaten and mixed it well together, I throw it in a new pot, and place it over a slow but steady fire." "As he said these things," so runs the story, "the cook uncovered the pot, and there issued forth a most delicious fragrance, perfuming the whole dining-hall, and overcoming the guests with delight." This is a point in gastronomic luxury to which Americans have not yet attained.

Although the perfume of roses was considered more choice than any other, it was frequently used when men were least in the state to enjoy it; for D'Orbessan states that slaves were made to burn it around their masters while sleeping.

If the essential oil of roses had been known in the time of Pliny, that author would have mentioned it among the most esteemed and precious perfumes. So far from this, however, he only speaks of the "Royal Perfume," so called because it was prepared expressly for the King of the Parthians. This was composed of the oil of Ben, an Arabian tree, with several aromatic substances. According to Langles, who has carefully examined a great number of oriental works, no writer, previous to the sixteenth century, has mentioned the essential oil of roses, although these flowers abounded at that time, and mention is made of rose-water as an agreeable perfume. Besides these negative proofs against the ancient existence of this perfume, Langles quotes several oriental historians, from which it seems evident that its discovery dates about the year 1612, and was owing entirely to accident.

According to Father Catron, in his *History of the Mogul Empire*, in the fêtes which the sultana Nourmahal gave to the great Mogul, Jehan-guire, their chief pleasure was sailing together in a canal which Nourmahal had filled with rose-water.

One day that the Emperor was thus sailing with Nourmahal, they perceived a sort of froth forming and floating upon the water. They drew it out, and perceived that it was the essential oil which the heat of the sun had disengaged from the water and collected together on the surface. The whole seraglio pronounced the perfume the most exquisite known in the Indies; and they immediately endeavored to imitate by art that which nature had made. Thus was discovered the essence, essential oil, otto, or attar of roses.

According to Langles, the word *A'ther*, *A'thr*, *or Othr*, which the Arabs, Turks, and Persians use to designate the essential oil of Roses without adding the name of that flower, is Arabic, and signifies perfume. It is necessary, the same author states, to recollect the distinction between *A'ther*, or *A'ther gul* and *gulab*, which is simply rose-water.

From the very small quantity congealed on the surface of the water, the manufacture is limited, and the cost of the article immense. Langles states that the rose-water is left exposed to the freshness of the night, and in the morning a very small quantity of attar is found collected on the surface.

Dr. Monro, according to Loudon, gives the manner of making the attar in Cashmere, which is apparently more simple, without the tedious process of distilling.

"The rose-petals are put into a wooden vessel with pure water, and exposed for several days to the heat of the sun. The oily particles, being disengaged by the heat, float upon the surface of the water, whence they are taken up from time to time by applying to them some very fine dry cotton wool. From this wool the oil is pressed into little bottles, which are immediately afterwards sealed hermetically."

Another method is, exposing the rose-water to heat, then suddenly cooling it, and collecting the drops of congealed oil which float upon the surface.

Bishop Heber describes the method used in India, which is very similar to that of Langles. The attar has the consistency of butter, and never becomes liquid except in the warmest weather.

Loudon states that "a wretched substitute for otto of roses is said to be formed by the apothecaries of Paris. The petals of *Rosa Damascena* are boiled in a large caldron of water along with as much hog's lard as will cover its surface with a thin stratum of grease. The oil of the rose-petals, on separating from them by boiling, unites with this grease, from which it is again separated by spirits of wine." A large portion of the attar imported into the United States is probably of this manufacture.

The quantity of genuine attar produced from a given weight of rose-petals is not always the same; it is very liable to vary according to the nature of the climate, the temperature of different seasons, the period of bloom at which the roses are picked, the process of manufacture, and the skill of the manufacturers. Generally, a hundred pounds of roses will scarcely produce a drachm of attar, sometimes only half a drachm, and at others a drachm and a half. Bishop Heber states that in India, at Ghazepoor, two hundred thousand well-grown roses are required to produce one rupee's (165 grains) weight of attar. The calyx is sometimes used with the petal, but as the oil of that contains little or no perfume, although it may increase the quantity of attar, it must sensibly weaken its properties.

The color of attar is generally green, sometimes lemon or rose color, and occasionally brownish. These differences in color are owing to the various processes of manufacture, and the different periods at which the roses are picked. The attar is prepared in Barbary, Syria, Arabia, Persia, India, in the island of Scio, at Fayoum, in Egypt, at Tunis, and many other places in the East. That made in Syria and Barbary is considered very inferior; while the best is made in Chyraz, Kerman, and Cashmere. In some parts of France and Italy it is also prepared, but in comparatively small quantities.

The attar is very costly, although not so dear as formerly. The French traveler, Tavernier, who visited Ispahan about the year 1666, stated that the price of attar at Chyraz rose and fell every year on account of the unequal produce of flowers; and that an ounce of that article sold, at one period, for ten tomans (about ninety-two dollars).

At the time another Frenchman, Chardin, traveled in Persia, some years after Tavernier, the attar was sometimes much higher. He states that forty pounds of rose-water were required to produce half a drachm of attar, an ounce of which sometimes sold in India for two hundred ecus. Langles states that in India half an ounce of attar is worth about forty dollars. Bishop Heber also speaks of its enormous price at Ghazepoor, where the variation in price is also very great, being, according to Langles, sometimes as low as eight dollars an ounce.

At one time, soon after its discovery, it was valued at about five times its weight in gold. Until quite recently, it was worth its weight in gold, but now sells in Paris for about one quarter that value.

Attar is rarely found pure in commerce; it is always more or less adulterated. In the countries where it is manufactured, they frequently increase the quantity of the attar by mixing scrapings of sandal-wood with the rose-petals during the process of distillation. Kæmpfer, a German writer, states this mode of adulteration to have been known a long time, and adds that the sandal-wood gives additional strength to the attar; but another author, who has also made some researches on the subject, asserts that the sandal-wood injures the delicacy of the attar, which is more sweet and agreeable when mild than when strong.

The quality as well as the quantity of attar which they obtain from roses depends upon the proportion of aroma which they contain; and this is found more developed at the South, and in a warm climate. The kinds of roses used in distillation have also a great influence on the quality of the attar. In Persia and the East, the Musk Rose is generally used, and the Damask is employed in France.

Although roses are distilled in large quantities at Paris for perfumery and for medical purposes, very little attar is made, because the proportion of the manufactured article to the roses required is, in that climate, extremely small; so small, in fact, that, according to one writer, five thousand parts in weight of rose-petals will scarcely produce one part of essential oil. This limited manufacture exists only at Grasse and Montpelier, in France, and at Florence, in Italy.

Some years since, the adulteration of attar was successfully practiced in the south of France by mixing with it the essence distilled from the leaves of the Rose Geranium (*Pelargonium capitatum*). This adulteration is very difficult to detect, because this last essence possesses the same properties as the attar; its odor is almost the same; like that, it is of a lemon color; it crystalizes at a lower temperature; and its density is very little greater.

The attar, when pure, is, beyond comparison, the most sweet and agreeable of all perfumes. Its fragrance is the most delicate conceivable, and equals that of the freshly expanded Rose. It is also so strong and penetrating, that a single drop, or as much as will attach itself to the point of a needle, is sufficient to perfume an apartment for several days; and if the small flask in which it is sold, although tightly corked and sealed, is placed in a drawer, it will perfume all the contents.

When in a congealed or crystalized state, the attar will liquefy at a slight heat; and if the flask is merely held in the hand, a few minutes will suffice to render it liquid. In the East much use is made of the attar, particularly in the harems. In Europe and America it is employed in the manufacture of cordials, and in the preparation of various kinds of perfumery.

Rose-water, or the liquid obtained from rose-petals by distillation, is very common, and is found in almost every country where the arts and luxuries of life have at all advanced.

Pliny tells us that rose-water was a favorite perfume of the Roman ladies, and the most luxurious used it even in their baths. This, however, must have been some preparation different from that now known as rose-water, and was probably a mere tincture of roses.

The ancients could have known nothing of rose-water,

for they were entirely ignorant of the art of distillation, which only came into practice after the invention of the alembic by the Arabs. Some attribute this discovery to Rhazes, an Arabian physician, who lived in the early part of the tenth century; and others attribute it to Avicenna, who lived at Chyraz, in the latter part of the same century. It is also attributed to Geber, a celebrated Arabian alchemist, who lived in Mesopotamia in the eighth century. Subsequent, therefore, to this discovery of the alembic, we find, according to Gmelin, in his history of the preparation of distilled waters, that the first notice of rose-water is by Aben-Zohar, a Jewish physician, of Seville, in Spain, who recommends it for diseases of the eye. From the Arabs, this invention passed among the Greeks and Romans, as we are informed by Actuarius, a writer of the eleventh or twelfth century.

In France, the first distillation of rose-water appears to have been made by Arnaud de Villeneuve, a physician, who lived in the latter part of the thirteenth century.

The Orientals made great use of this water in various ways in their houses, and in the purification of their temples when they thought they had been profaned by any other worship than that of Mahomet. There are many anecdotes told by historians of the use of rose-water by the Sultans on various occasions; and several of these, as Chateaubriand remarks, are stories worthy of the East. It is related of Saladin, that when he took Jerusalem from the Crusaders, in 1187, he would not enter the Mosque of Omar, which had been converted into a church by the Christians, until the walls and courts had been thoroughly washed and purified with rose-water brought from Damascus. Five hundred camels, it is stated, were scarcely sufficient to convey all the rose-water used for this purpose. An Arabian writer tells us that the princes of the family of Saladin, hastening to Jerusalem to worship Allah, Malek-Abdul, and his nephew, Taki-Eddin, distinguished themselves above all others. The latter repaired with all his followers to the "Chapel of the Holy Cross," and taking a broom himself, he swept all the dirt from the floor, washed the walls and the ceiling several times with pure water, and then washed them with rose-water; having thus cleansed and purified the place, he distributed large alms to the poor.

Bibars, the fourth Sultan of the Mameluke dynasty, who reigned from 1260 to 1277, caused the Caaba of the temple of Mecca to be washed with rose-water.

Mahomet II., after the capture of Constantinople, in 1453, would not enter the Mosque of St. Sophia, which had been formerly used as a church, until he had caused it to be washed with rose-water.

It is stated by a French historian that the greatest display of gorgeous magnificence at that period was made in 1611, by the Sultan Ahmed I., at the dedication of the new Caaba, which had been built or repaired at his expense; amber and aloes were burnt in profusion, and, in the extravagance of Eastern language, oceans of rose-water were set afloat, for washing the courts and interior surface of the walls. Rose-water is by no means so generally used now as for a few hundred years subsequent to its invention. In France, during the reign of Philip Augustus, it was a necessary article at court. It was formerly the custom to carry large vases filled with rose-water to baptisms. Illustrating this custom, Bayle relates a story of Rousard, the French poet: "It nearly happened that the day of his birth was also that of his death; for when he was carried from the Chateau de La Poissonière to the church of the place to be baptized, the nurse who carried him carelessly let him fall; his fall, however, was upon the grass and flowers, which received him softly; it so happened, that a young lady, who carried a vase filled with rose-water and a collection of flowers, in her haste to aid in helping the child, overturned on his head a large part of the rose-water. This incident was considered a presage of the good odor with which France would one day be filled by the flowers of his learned writings."

At one time rose-water was largely consumed in the preparation of food and the seasoning of various dishes. In the "Private Life of the French," it is mentioned that in the fourteenth century, the Comte d'Etampes gave a feast in which a large part of the dishes and even the chestnuts were prepared with rose-water. It is still used to flavor various dishes, but its principal use is in affections of the eyelids, or as a perfume for the toilet. The principal consumption of rose-water is, however, in the East, where the inhabitants are very fond of perfumes. In Persia a very large quantity is made annually for domestic use. They deem it an excellent beverage mixed with pure water.

The Corinth Grape, mixed with rose-water, and a slight infusion of spices, is the nectar so much in vogue among the Greeks of Morea. The Persians, according to Lebruyn, sprinkle with rose-water those who visit them. They also make it an important article of commerce; large quantities are sent to different parts of the East, and entire cargoes are sometimes shipped to India.

In Egypt, the nobles and wealthy inhabitants consume large quantities of rose-water; they scatter it over their divans and other places where they spend their time; they also offer it with confectionery to their visitors.

The custom of offering rose-water to a guest is alluded to by Shakespeare, who makes one of his characters in Padua say:

"What is it your honor will command?
Let one attend him with a silver bason
Full of *rose-water*, and bestrewed with flowers."

Almost all the rose-water used in Egypt is distilled in the province of Fayoum, from the pale rose. "About the middle of February, in Fayoum," says a French writer, "they pluck the roses every morning before sunrise, while the dew is yet upon them; they then place them immediately in the alembic, not allowing them to become dry or heated by remaining too long a time without distillation. This lucrative branch of manufacture has not escaped the monopoly of Mehemet Ali. No private individual can now distil roses in Egypt, and those who cultivate them are obliged to sell the petals to government at a low price. The value of all the rose-water distilled in Fayoum, annually, is estimated at 50,000 or 60,000 francs." Of the profusion with which rose-water is used in India, some idea may be formed from the narrative of Bishop Heber, who was shown, in the ruins of the palace of Ghazepoor, a deep trench round an octagonal platform of blue, red, and white mosaic pavement. This trench, he was told, was filled with rose-water when the Nawâb and his friends were feasting in the middle. "The ancient oil of roses," according to Loudon, "is obtained by bruising fresh rose-petals, mixing them with four times their weight of olive oil, and leaving them in a sand-heat for two days. If the red Rose of Provence is used, the oil is said to imbibe no odor; but if the petals of pale roses are employed, it becomes perfumed. This preparation was celebrated among the ancients. Pliny says that, according to Homer, roses were macerated for their oil in the time of the Trojans. The oil is chiefly used for the hair, and is generally sold in perfumers' shops, both in France and England, under the name of *L'huile antique de Rose.*"

Spirit of roses is made by distilling rose-petals with a small quantity of spirits of wine, and forms an agreeable article for external applications. The green leaves of the sweet-brier are sometimes, in France, steeped in spirits of wine to impart a fragrance; and in England they are frequently used to flavor cowslip wine.

As the petals of the rose preserve their fragrance for a long time after being dried, many are in the habit of making, annually, little bags filled with them. These, being placed in a drawer or wardrobe, impart an agreeable perfume to the linen or clothing with which they may come in contact. The petals can be obtained from almost any garden in sufficient quantity for this purpose, and can be dried by the process mentioned hereafter. The confectioners, distillers, and perfumers of France draw from the Rose a part of their perfumes, particularly from *R. Damascena*, and *R. centifolia*, in fixing their sweet odors in sugar-plums, creams, ices, oils, pomatum, essences, and fragrant powders.

The petals of the Rose, after being freshly picked and bruised in a marble mortar, until they are reduced to a sort of paste, are employed in the preparation of different kinds of confectionery. Of this paste the French also make little perfume balls of the size of a pea. They are made round in the same manner as pills, and before becoming hard, they are pierced with a needle and strung on a piece of silk. In a little while they become hard like wood, assume a brownish color, and emit a delightful perfume. This rose scent continues very long, and one writer remarks that he has known a necklace made in this style, possess, at the end of twenty-five years, as strong a perfume as when first made.

In Great Britain, in the vicinity of the large cities, and in many private gardens, the flowers are gathered for making rose-water or for drying as perfumes. In Holland, the Dutch *hundred-leaved* and common *cabbage rose* are grown extensively at Noordwich, between Leyden and Haarlem, and the dried leaves are sent to Amsterdam and Constantinople. In France, the Provence Rose is extensively cultivated near the town of Provence, about sixty miles south-east of Paris, and also at Fontenay aux Roses, near Paris, for the manufacture of rose-water, or for exportation in a dried state. The petals of the Provence Rose (*Rosa Gallica*) are the only ones that are said to gain additional fragrance in drying; all the other varieties losing in this process more or less of their perfume. A French writer states, that apothecaries employ both pale and red roses; the pale give more perfume, while the red keep the longer.

Loudon states that "the petals of roses ought always to be gathered as soon as the flower is fully expanded; and the gathering should never be deferred until it has begun to fade, because, in the latter case, the petals are not only discolored, but weakened in their perfume and their medical properties. They should be immediately separated from the calyx, and the claws of the petals pinched off; they are then dried in the shade, if the weather is dry and warm, or by a stove in a room, if the season is humid, care being taken, in either case, not to spread them on the ground, but on a platform raised two or three feet above it. The drying should be conducted expeditiously, because it has been found that slowly dried petals do not exhale near so much odor as those which have been dried quickly, which is also the case with hay, sweet herbs, and odoriferous vegetables generally. After the petals are dried, they are freed from any sand, dust, or eggs of insects which may adhere to them, by shaking them and rubbing them gently in a fine sieve. After this, the petals are put into close vessels, from which the air is excluded, and which are kept in a dry, airy situation.

"As it is extremely difficult to free the rose-petals entirely from the eggs of insects, they are taken out of these vessels two or three times a year, placed in sieves, rubbed, cleaned, and replaced."

I have been careful to give the details of the above process, because it may be useful to those who embark extensively in the cultivation of roses for the exportation of petals in a dried state. We should suppose that rose-petals produced in this latitude, where the Rose has a long period of hibernation, would produce more perfume, and be more valuable in a dried state than those grown under the tropics. The Provence and Damask Rose are both known to succeed well here, and to produce abundant flowers. Their fragrance is unsurpassed, and our summer's sun would be abundantly sufficient to dry the petals without any artificial heat. It is not too much to hope that the attention of our cultivators may yet be directed to this subject, and that the manufacture of rose-water and the preparation of dried petals may yet be an important branch of domestic industry, and form an important addition to the list of exported articles.

CHAPTER XV.

THE MEDICAL PROPERTIES OF THE ROSE.

We have hitherto viewed the Rose as the chief ornament of our gardens, and if we have found it abounding with charms of fragrance and beauty, we shall now find it occupying a prominent place in Materia Medica. Some authors have, with a degree of exaggeration, endeavored to make its medical as brilliant as its floral reputation. Rosenberg, in his work on the Rose, makes it a specific in every disease, and even attributes to it supernatural virtues.

In the opinion of most medical men, the medicinal properties of the Rose are about the same in all the kinds, while some writers assert that the *Rosa Gallica* is superior to all others in a greater or less degree. We will mention those principally used in medicine, and the properties which are especially attributed to each.

The most valuable properties of the Rose reside in its

petals, and in order to preserve these properties, it is highly essential that the petals should be quickly and perfectly dried. Those of the Provence Rose (*Rosa Gallica*) have an astringent and somewhat bitter taste, and are tonic and astringent in their effects.

According to an analysis recently made in France, they contain, besides vegetable matter and essential oil, a portion of gallic acid, coloring matter, albumen, tannin, some salts, with a base of potash or of chalk, silex, and oxide of iron. A small dose in powder strengthens the stomach and assists digestion. Their prolonged use will sometimes cause a slight constipation of the bowels, while in a much stronger dose they act as purgatives.

The *conserve* of the Provence Rose has much reputation in France for the treatment of all chronic affections of the bowels, caused by weakness and inactivity of the digestive organs; it is also employed in colic, in diarrhœa, in cases of hemorrhage and leucorrhœa.

The conserve of any variety of roses is considered excellent in cases of cold or catarrh. It is prepared by bruising in a mortar the petals with their weight in sugar, and moistening them with a little rose-water, until the whole forms a homogeneous mass. Some receipts prescribe powdered petals mixed with an equal part of sugar; others direct to use two layers of sugar, and only one layer of pulverized petals.

Opoix, a physician of Provence, states that the true Rose of Provence has a more sweet and penetrating fragrance than the same rose grown elsewhere, and even goes so far as to say that it has acquired properties which it does not possess in its native country, the Caucasus. On account of the supposed superior qualities of this rose, the citizens of Provence, in 1807, addressed a petition to government to encourage in their territory the cultivation of the true Provence Rose, by giving it the preference in all the hospitals and military dispensaries. This gave rise to a discussion between two French chemists, but without deciding the fact whether the *Rosa Gallica* was superior in medical properties to any other rose. It seems to be acknowledged that those cultivated at Provence were superior to the same kind grown elsewhere, and this superiority is attributed by some to the presence of iron in the soil about that city. It was probably owing, also, to the very careful cultivation practiced there. The petals are used extensively in several medical preparations, as the sugar of roses, the ointment of roses, the treacle of roses, etc. Rose-water is, however, more extensively used in medicine than any other preparation of the rose. This water, when manufactured from *Rósa Gallica*, or any other of the section of *Centifoliæ*, is employed internally as an astringent, and is sometimes mixed with other medicines to destroy their disagreeable smell and taste. In external applications, it is used principally for affections of the eyes, either alone or with some ointment.

The *alcoholic tincture of roses*, or spirit of roses, before mentioned, which was formerly given as a stimulus in many cases, has now fallen very much into disuse, medical opinion being very much against the employment of any alcoholic medicines excepting in very rare cases.

The *syrup of roses*, manufactured from the pale or Damask Rose, is sometimes employed as a purgative, and was once highly esteemed and recommended as a mild laxative. It is now, however, scarcely considered purgative, and its laxative properties are probably owing in a great measure to the senna and other articles which enter into its preparation.

The *electuary of roses*, which is now no longer used, was also probably indebted for its medical qualities to the addition of scammony, a very strong purgative.

Vinegar of roses is made by simply infusing dried rose-petals in the best distilled vinegar, to which they communicate their perfume. It is used for cooking and for the toilet, and for headaches, when applied in the same way as common vinegar. The ancients prepared this vinegar, and also the wine and oil of roses, which are no longer used.

Honey of roses is made by beating up rose-petals with a very small portion of boiling water; the liquid, after being filtered, is boiled with honey. This is esteemed for sore throats, for ulcers in the mouth, and for anything that is benefited by the use of honey.

The fruit of the rose is said also to possess some astringent properties; the pulp of the fruit of the wild varieties, particularly of the dog rose, after being separated from the seeds and beaten up in a mortar with sugar, makes a sort of conserve, formerly known in medicine under the name of Cynorrhodon.

Children in the country sometimes eat these fruits after they have attained perfect maturity, and have been somewhat mellowed by the frost; they then lose their pungent taste, and become a little sweet. Belanger, a French writer, who traveled in Persia in 1825, found in that country a rose whose fruit was very agreeably flavored. The apple-bearing rose (*R. villosa pomifera*) produces the largest fruit of all, and is the best adapted for preserving; but an English writer remarks that the fruit of *R. systyla* and *R. arvensis*, although of a smaller size, bears a higher flavor than that of any other species. Rose-buds, like the fruit, are also frequently preserved in sugar, and pickled in vinegar. Tea is sometimes made of the leaves of the rose, which are also eaten readily by the domestic animals.

The ends of the young shoots of the sweet-brier, deprived of their bark and foliage, and cut into short pieces, are sometimes candied and sold by the confectioners.

The Dog Rose takes its name from the virtue which the ancients attributed to its root as a cure for hydrophobia. The heathen deities themselves, according to Pliny, revealed this marvelous property, in dream, to a mother whose son had been bitten by a dog affected with this terrible disease.

The excrescences frequently found on the branches of the Rose, and particularly on those of the wild varieties, known to druggists by the Arabic name of *Bédeguar*, and which resemble in form a little bunch of moss, partake equally of the astringent properties of the Rose. These excrescences are caused by the puncture of a little insect, known to naturalists as the *Cynips rosæ*, and, occasionally, nearly the same effects are produced by other insects.

CHAPTER XVI.

GENERAL REMARKS.

The name of the Rose is very similar in most languages, but of its primitive derivation very little or nothing is known. It is *rhodon* in Greek; *rhos*, in Celtic; *rosa*, in Latin, Italian, Spanish, Portuguese, Hungarian, and Polish; *rose*, in French, Saxon, and English; *rosen*, in German; *roose*, in Dutch; *rhoshd*, in Sclavonic; *ros*, in Irish; *ruoze*, in Bohemian; *ouasrath*, in Arabic; *nisrin*, in Turkish; *chabhatzeleth*, in Hebrew; and *gul*, in Persian. These are the various names by which the flower has been known from very early times, and a strong resemblance can be traced through all. The Latin name, *rosa*, also forms a component part of terms used to designate several other things.

The name of *rosary* was given to a string of beads used in the Romish Church to represent a certain number of prayers; it was instituted about the year 667, but was not much used until Peter the Hermit excited the Christian nations to the Crusade, about 1096. Dominique, a Romish saint, established, in 1207, the brotherhood of the Rosary, and the festival of the Rose was instituted in 1571 by Pope Pius V., in thanksgiving for the victory gained by the Christians over the Turks at Lepante. Subsequent popes gave to that ceremony more eclat, and caused it to be established in Spain. The name of *rosary* was formerly also given to the vessel used in distilling rose-water. The Rose has also given the idea of new forms of beauty in architecture and the arts. A rose is sometimes sculptured in the centre of each face of a Corinthian capital. It is also frequently seen in iron castings for the banisters of the stone steps of a house, and it is sometimes displayed upon the pavement in front of some splendid mansion. This, however, is rare in the United States, although frequent in Europe.

Among all the imitations of the Rose, none can compare with those painted on glass, some of which can be found in the windows of celebrated European Cathedrals in Canterbury, Cologne, Milan, Rheims, St. Denis, and others. We can scarcely imagine anything more beautifully soft than these paintings on glass, as seen from the interior of a church, in the rich light of a glowing sunset; the Rose thus painted seems to possess all the freshness and beauty of the real flower.

The nave of the Cathedral of Paris, besides twenty-four large windows, is lighted by three others, large and magnificent, in the shape of a Rose, which are each forty feet in diameter. The paintings on glass which ornament these windows were executed in the 13th century, and still retain their fresh and bright colors: that over the grand entrance represents the signs of the zodiac, and the agricultural labors of each month.

In heraldry, the rose frequently forms part of a shield, in full bloom, with a bud in the centre, and with five points to imitate thorns; it is an emblem of beauty and of nobility acquired with difficulty.

The Golden Rose was considered so honorable a present, that none but monarchs were worthy to receive it.

In the 11th century, the Pope introduced the custom of blessing a golden Rose, which he presented to some church, or to some prince or princess, as an especial mark of his favor.

In 1096, the Pope Urban II. gave a Golden Rose to the Comte d'Anjou. Alexander III. sent one to Louis, King of France, in acknowledgment of the attentions of that prince during the Pope's visit to France, as stated in a letter which he wrote the King.

"In accordance with the custom of our ancestors, in carrying a rose of gold in their hands on Dimanche Lætare, we do not think we can present it to one who merits it more than yourself, from your devotion to the Church and to ourselves."

Pope John, in 1415, sent the Golden Rose to the Emperor Sigismund. Martin V., in 1418, sent another to the same prince. Pius II., in 1461, sent one to Thomas Palelogue, Emperor of Constantinople. Henry VIII., of England, before his separation from the Church of Rome, received the Golden Rose twice; the first from Julius II., and the second from Leo X.; and in 1842, the Pope's Nuncio Capaccini presented it to Donna Maria, Queen of Portugal. Isabella, Queen of Spain, was presented with it a few years since.

The public ceremony of blessing the Rose was not instituted until 1366, by Urban V.: that pontiff, wishing to give a particular mark of his esteem to Joanna, Queen of Sicily, solemnly blessed a Golden Rose, which he sent her, and made at the same time a decree, that a similar one should be consecrated every year. For fifty or sixty years, the Pope gave the Rose to princes who came to Rome; and it was the custom to give 500 louis to the officer who carried it for the Pope. The Rose, in its intrinsic value, was, however, sometimes worth double that sum.

We have thus given all the information we have been able to collect respecting the history of the Rose.

We shall feel abundantly gratified if the facts and anecdotes we have cited shall tend to enhance the already growing interest in this flower; and by thus connecting it with the lore of antiquity, cast around it a bright halo of pleasant associations.

Among the various riches of the garden, there are many flowers of great attractions: some we admire for their beautiful forms, others for their brilliant colors, and others again for their delightful fragrance; and we scarcely know which to pronounce the most pleasing. But whatever may be our feelings of admiration for these beautiful flowers, a desire for something still more beautiful draws us to the Rose, and compels us to pronounce it superior to all its rivals. It is the Rose alone that never fatigues, that always exhibits some new beauty, and that is never affected by fashion; for while Dahlias and other flowers have had their hour of favor, and have passed out of notice, the Rose has been a favorite for some three thousand years, and is still the first and most beautiful,—the *chef d'œuvre* of the vegetable kingdom.

The Rose is rendered a favorite by many pleasant associations. It has been the cherished flower of the ancient poets, and with modern poets it has lost none of its charms, but is still apostrophized and made an object of frequent comparison. With the ancients, it was, as we have seen, the ornament of their festivals, their altars, and their tombs: it was the emblem of beauty, youth, modesty, and innocence, and was full of tender sentiment and pleasant images. A French writer, in a somewhat more extravagant vein of laudation, says, "Its name alone gives birth in all sensible minds to a crowd of pleasant thoughts, while, at the same time, it excites a sensation of the most delightful pleasures, and the most sweet enjoyments." The name of "Queen of Flowers," has been given to the Rose, almost from time immemorial; but this name is particularly applicable to the *R. centifolia* and the hybrids from it. Yet the little, modest wild rose, found only in woods and hedges, adorns the solitude where it grows, and possesses for many a charm not surpassed by that of any of the cultivated varieties: its regularly formed corolla, of a soft and delicate color, combines in its simplicity many an attraction not found in the most beautiful flowers of the garden; and late in the season, when the fields are stripped of their verdure, the landscape is enlivened by the bright appearance of its red, coral-like fruit.

The beauty of the Rose has preserved it and its reputation for many ages. The most populous nations, the largest cities, the most wealthy and powerful kingdoms, have disappeared from the earth, or have been involved in the revolutions and subversions of empires, while a simple flower has escaped them all, and still remains to tell its story. It has seen a hundred generations succeed each other, and pass away; it has traveled through ages without changing its destiny or losing its character: the homage rendered and the love borne it have been always the same: now, as in the earliest periods of the world's history, it is decreed the first place in the floral kingdom. In these days, as in those of antiquity, it is *par excellence*, the Queen of Flowers, because it is always the most beautiful, and because no other flower can furnish half its charms. To elegance and beauty of form it unites the freshness and brilliance of the most agreeable colors, and, as if nature had showered upon it all her most precious gifts, it adds to its other qualities a delightful perfume, which alone would suffice to entitle it to a distinguished place among the beautiful and pleasant things of the vegetable kingdom.

FLORA'S CHOICE.

When Flora, from her azure home,
Came gently down to grace the earth,
She called around her every sprite
To which the sunny air gives birth,
And bade them search each distant realm
Of tropic heat or temperate clime,
From cold New England's rocky hills
To Santa Crusian groves of lime,
And bring each floweret, rich and rare,
For her to choose her favorite there.

Quick flew the sprites o'er land and sea,
Through cloud, and mist, and storm afar,
Catching, with rapid, eagle glance,
The beauties of each opening flower:
From Alpine heights they bore a prize,
From Persia and from Hindostan;
For many a bud of beauty rare
They searched the central, flowery land,
And, filled with treasures rich and sweet,
They hasten'd to their mistress' feet.

Camellia, with its lustrous white
And glossy leaves of emerald hue;

Verbena, with its brilliant red,
And Heath just touch'd with mountain dew;
Azalea, whose aerial form
Seems scarcely of terrestrial birth;
And Cinerara's purple star,
Gracing full well its mother earth;
And many a flower from tropic skies
Strove mingled there to gain the prize.

But not the richest tropic blooms,
Cull'd from the fairest climes on earth,
Could vie with nature's fairest flower,
Of Iran's sun-clad soil the birth;
Though clothed in rich and gorgeous hues,
They bore no charm of fragrance there,
In form and color, sweetness, grace—
None with the Rose could once compare:
She bore the palm in Flora's eyes,
Who to the Rose adjudged the prize.

S. B. P.

THE ROSE.

Though many a flower has graced the lay
And formed the theme of poets' song—
Has gently flowed in Grecian phrase,
Or tripped upon the Roman's tongue;
Yet, still, in ancient song and story
The Rose shines forth in beauty rare,
Enveloped with a halo bright,
And made so glorious, rich, and fair,

That all the flowers must yield their seat,
And lay their beauty at its feet.
Anacreon sang its primal birth,
Old Homer praised its form of grace,
Catullus boasted of its charms,
Horace, its richly tinted face:
In fair Italia's glowing words,
Tasso and Metastasio sang;
And 'mong the groves of far Cathay
The Persian Hafiz' accents rang.
The flowing tones of old Castile,
From Camoens and Sannazar,
And in our own pure English tongue
It was the signal note of war;
In many a poet's verse its beauty shone,—
Milton, the Bard of Avon, and the Great Unknown.
High valued were its flowers bright
By Helle's maids of yore;
It graced their scenes of festive glee
In the classic vales of Arcady,
And all the honors bore;
And shed its fragrance on the breeze
That swept through academic grove,
Where sages with their scholars rove—
The land of Pericles.
In the sunny clime of Suristan,
On India's burning shore,
Amid the Brahmin's sacred shades,
Or in the wreaths that Persian maids,
Sporting in bright and sunny glades
In graceful beauty wore;
Upon the banks of Jordan's stream
Still flowing softly on,
Where Judah's maidens once did lave,
Or where the lofty cedars wave,
On time-worn Lebanon;

The Rose is still most rich and sweet,
And wears the crown for beauty meet.
I have basked in the beauty of southern climes,
And wandered through groves of palm and limes,
Where dark-eyed Spanish girls
Would linger in their myrtle bowers,—
With garlands rich of orange flowers
Would weave their raven curls,
And fasten 'mid their lustrous hair
The fire-fly's glittering light,
Which, brighter than the diamond's sheen,
Bursts on the dazzled sight.
But yet I would not give for these,
Produce of tropic sun and breeze—
For all the flowers in beauty there—
The Rose our northern maidens wear.
I've crossed the Andes' lofty height,
Its mountains, forest-crowned,
And 'mong the devious, tangled paths
Of tropic thickets wound.
In fair Aragua's fertile vale,
In Hayti's fields of bloom,
I've marked the prickly Cactus tribe
Its richest tints assume.
I've passed through fragrant Coffee groves,
By the tall Bucara tree,
And by the Cocoa and the Palm,
With the Trupeol warbling free;
Upon the flower-clad turf, and where
The rich Orchidia climbs in air.
But not 'mid all this gorgeous bloom,
By tropic climate wove,
Nor Florida's rich Magnolia
And fragrant Orange grove;
Nor the graceful vines of southern France,
Nor Italy's fair bowers,

Nor England's lofty domes of glass
All filled with gorgeous flowers;
Nor in our own wide prairie land,
With bud and bloom on every hand,
Is there a single flower that grows
Can vie in beauty with the Rose.

Then seek, in southern, tropic air,
And in our northern glade,
And in the bright and gay parterre,
And by the forest shade,
Where every flower, and leaf, and tree,
In graceful blending met,
Presents new beauty to the eye,
Of azure or of jet;
And take each blossom, rich and rare,
Which thou may'st find in beauty there;
Combine their color, form, and grace,
And each unpleasant tint erase;
Then recreate the loveliest flower
That e'er shed fragrance in a bower;
Let all its sweets and charms unclose;
It cannot equal yet the Rose.

S. B. P.

INDEX.

VARIETIES AND SPECIES.

www.ingramcontent.com/pod-product-compliance
Lightning Source LLC
LaVergne TN
LVHW011207110826
845150LV00006B/1351